ROBERT E. LEE
SLEPT HERE

D1495591

ROBERT E. LEE SLEPT HERE

CIVIL WAR INNS AND DESTINATIONS— A GUIDE FOR THE DISCERNING TRAVELER

Written and Photographed by

CHUCK LAWLISS

BALLANTINE BOOKS

NEW YORK

Sale of this book without a front cover may be unauthorized. If this book is coverless, it may have been reported to the publisher as "unsold or destroyed" and neither the author nor the publisher may have received payment for it.

A Ballantine Book
Published by The Ballantine Publishing Group

Copyright © 1998 by Chuck Lawliss

All rights reserved under International and Pan-American Copyright Conventions. Published in the United States by The Ballantine Publishing Group, a division of Random House, Inc., New York, and simultaneously in Canada by Random House of Canada Limited, Toronto.

http://www.randomhouse.com

Library of Congress Catalog Card Number: 98-96013

ISBN: 0-345-42156-6

Cover design by Dreu Pennington-McNeil
Cover photos: Background photo and General Robert E. Lee courtesy of Edward Vebell; *Loyd Hall, Oak Square Plantation, North Bend Plantation* courtesy of Chuck Lawliss; *Perryville Battlefield State Historic Site* courtesy of the Kentucky Department of Travel Development; *Garth Woodside Mansion* courtesy of Jessie Walker; *Burnside Bridge, Antietam* © Patrick Soran/Maryland Office of Tourism Development

Book design by H. Roberts Design

Manufactured in the United States of America

First Edition: May 1998

10 9 8 7 6 5 4 3 2 1

Contents

Introduction

People were visiting Civil War battlefields even before the Civil War was over. Almost before the smoke cleared at Manassas, people were walking around Henry House Hill and peeping in the window of the Stone House. It was the same at Gettysburg. Men and women came to walk the battlefield and see Little Round Top and Devil's Den and the "little clump of trees" where Pickett's Charge was thrown back. People are curious, but it is more than that. They want a sense of what it was like to be part of a great event, to be part of history.

Interest in the Civil War still grows. It is greater now than it was in the 1960s when we celebrated the centennial, greater than it was ten years ago, and it is a good bet it will be still greater in another ten years. The Civil War shaped the America we know today.

The war also greatly affected the people who fought in it. The great Supreme Court justice and Civil War captain Oliver Wendell Holmes put it best: "We have shared the incommunicable experience of war. We have felt, we still feel, the passion of life to its top . . . in our youth our hearts were touched with fire." If a century after the fact, we can't be touched by that fire, we can at least feel its warmth.

One way to enrich and intensify our Civil War experience is to stay at an inn that was connected to the war, an inn owned and operated by people who love their place and its link to the past. Staying in such a place can add a new dimension to your trip. For a moment you brush up against history. It's a nice feeling.

This book brings together Civil War sites and the inns that are connected to them in some way. This will allow your experience of one to enhance your experience of the other. When you're exploring the Shenandoah Valley, for instance, stay for a night at the house in Charles Town, West Virginia, where Grant and Sheridan met to plan Sheridan's Valley campaign. At Antietam, stay at the farmhouse on the battlefield where Longstreet made his headquarters. Wouldn't you know Jefferson Davis better if you stayed at the Mississippi plantation where he spent his youth? Wouldn't a visit to a great plantation let you experience the life that has gone with the wind?

When I am traveling to gather information and take photographs for a book or an article on the Civil War, I make a point of staying at inns. Innkeepers are a great source of information. They know what's around, how to get there, and whom I should talk to when I arrive. Furthermore, when traveling by yourself it's a pleasure to chat with your hosts at the end of a long day.

How to Use This Book

All but a handful of the inns described in this book were visited by the author, and the others were visited by his friends. Although the inns range from the rustic to the manorial and from inexpensive to very expensive, all are recommended.

To avoid disappointment there are a few things to remember. One, make reservations. Inns are small and their guest rooms fill up fast, particularly in season (summer in the North, spring and fall in the South).

Two, if you have special requirements, discuss them with the innkeeper when you make your reservation. This is particularly important if you are traveling with someone who requires a wheelchair. Also, many inns have restrictions on pets and young children.

All inns provide breakfast to their guests, and the majority provide a full breakfast; only the exceptions are noted in the individual listings.

Inn rates change. For this reason a simple code is used instead of the rate quoted when this book was being prepared:

$$$: Expensive
$$: Moderate
$: Inexpensive

THE NORTH

AND THE

BORDER STATES

NEW HAMPSHIRE

The Chase House

The Chase House

Cornish, New Hampshire

The war was costing the Union $2.5 million a day by 1863, a price that would total more than $6 billion before it was over. The man responsible for that money was Salmon Chase, a former Ohio governor with no financial background who competed with Lincoln for the Republican presidential candidacy. When Chase lost, Lincoln appointed him secretary of the treasury.

Lincoln valued Chase's competence and the political savvy that enabled him to get finance bills through Congress. But their friendship ended when Lincoln learned Chase had secretly agreed to run against him in 1864. However, Lincoln later appointed him chief justice of the Supreme Court, a position he held until his death in 1873.

Chase was born in this Federal-style house, in what is now the dining room, in 1808.

The Chase House has been restored and now is a handsome inn, located on the Connecticut River and shaded by stately trees. The furnishings are elegant and the full breakfast served up by innkeeper Barbara Lewis prepares guests for a morning of sightseeing.

Address: Rte. 12A, Cornish, NH 03745; tel: 603-675-5391.
Accommodations: Six double rooms, four with private baths, and two rooms with shared bath.
Amenities: Air-conditioning, off-street parking, canoeing, hiking, and cross-country skiing on trails on the property.
Rates: $$–$$$. Visa, MasterCard, and personal checks.
Restrictions: No children under twelve, no pets, no smoking.

OHIO

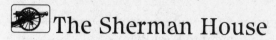 # The Sherman House

Lancaster, Ohio

Charles Sherman, a young Connecticut lawyer, came to Lancaster in 1810, moved his family into this small frame house, and established a law practice. His son, William Tecumseh Sherman, was born in 1820.

Nine years later, Charles died, leaving his widow with eleven children. A neighbor, Thomas Ewing, offered to take the "smartest" of the boys: William. "I was taken by Mr. Ewing and put on a par with his own children," he later recalled.

Ewing was elected to the U.S. Senate in 1830, and later

held several cabinet posts. In 1836 he secured "Cump," as the boy was called, an appointment to West Point.

In 1850, Sherman married his guardian's daughter, Ellen Ewing, who would bear him eight children. He resigned from the army in 1853 and was involved in banking and real estate. He found his niche when he became superintendent of a military academy in Louisiana, where he stayed until the state seceded. Sherman returned to the army in 1861 and went on to fame.

The house today has an 1816 addition, which contains Judge Ewing's study and the family parlor. On the second floor is a re-creation of Sherman's field tent with war artifacts and family memorabilia.

The Sherman House, 137 E. Main St., Lancaster, OH 43130, is open April through mid-December, Tuesday–Sunday, 1:00–4:00. Open by appointment at other times. Admission is $2.50 for adults, $1 for children six to seventeen. For information phone 740-654-9923.

Shaw's Inn

Lancaster, Ohio

Picture a tree-shaded square in a midwestern town with a gazebo where a brass band plays concerts on soft summer nights. Add a charming inn and a good restaurant and you have Shaw's in Lancaster, Ohio, the boyhood home of William T. Sherman, the Union general who made "Marching Through Georgia" his tune.

The inn, owned by Bruce and Nancy Cork, has been a landmark here since the early 1800s, greeting such distinguished guests as Henry Clay and Daniel Webster. The story goes that Rudolph Pitcher, a previous owner, lost the tavern in a poker game. The restaurant, built in 1939 on the site of the original, merits three stars from the *Mobil Guide* and high marks from the *Zagat Survey*.

The Sherman House is only a half-block away and a Georgian mansion is just across the street. General Sherman's birthday, February 8, is an event at Shaw's, and guests and neighbors enjoy attending the festivities in period costumes.

Address: 123 N. Broad St., Lancaster, OH 43130; tel: 614-654-1842 or 800-654-2477; fax: 614-654-7032.

Accommodations: Fifteen double rooms and seven suites, all with private baths.

Amenities: Air-conditioning, off-street parking; rooms have phones, cable TV, hair dryers, suites have whirlpool baths.

Rates: $$–$$$. Visa, MasterCard, and personal checks.

Restrictions: No pets.

KENTUCKY

Shaker Village of Pleasant Hill

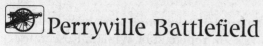 # Perryville Battlefield

Perryville, Kentucky

Confederate General Braxton Bragg invaded Kentucky in the fall of 1862, and Union General Don Carlos Buell moved east from Louisville to prevent him from joining up with General Kirby Smith and his army from across the Mississippi. There was a drought, both armies were seeking water, and neither side knew how close it was to the other. They blundered into each other here, at Doctor's Creek, on October 8.

The leading column, commanded by Union Brigadier General Philip Sheridan, first skirmished near the creek; then Bragg, unaware that he was outnumbered three to one, struck the Union left. He was repelled, but Buell's reluctance to press the attack cost him an important victory. Half of his army took no part in the battle, and Bragg got away unmolested. The battle cost 4,211 Federal and 3,396 Confederate casualties.

By the end of the month, both armies were back in Tennessee, where Buell was soon replaced by William Rosecrans. Perryville was the last battle in Kentucky, the Confederacy's last serious attempt to gain control of the state. All three Confederate invasions that fall had foundered—Earl Van Dorn and Sterling Price at Corinth, Mississippi, Robert E. Lee in Maryland, and now Bragg in Kentucky.

The Perryville Battlefield State Shrine is reached from the Bluegrass Pkwy. by taking Exit 59, then going twenty-four miles south on U.S. 127 through Harrodsburg to Danville. Then take the 127/150 bypass, go right (west) on U.S. 150, drive nine miles to Perryville, and go north on KY 1920 to the battlefield. The 250-acre park looks much as it did at the time of the battle. Still standing are the **Crawford House,** Bragg's headquarters, and the **Bottom House,** the center of some of the heaviest fighting. A large map of the battle is in the small museum at the **Visitor Center**. Open April through October, 9:00–5:00, and other times by appointment. The battle is reenacted annually on the weekend closest to October 8. Admission is $2 for adults, $1 for children. For information phone 606-332-8631.

The whole town of **Perryville** (population 815), a National Register district, looks much as it did when the battle was fought nearby. For information phone 606-332-1862.

🏛 Shaker Village of Pleasant Hill

Harrodsburg, Kentucky

Shaker Village, once the home of a religious community, was located on a turnpike that was used by both Union and Confederate troops throughout the war, particularly during the 1862 Kentucky campaign. The Shakers were Unionists and abolitionists, but their pacifism kept them out of the conflict.

They were hospitable to both armies as they marched through the village, and nursed the wounded after the Battle of Perryville. Shaker Village, which was founded in 1805, has been restored and twenty-seven original buildings are open. Guests stay in "family houses" and the meetinghouse. In the Shaker tradition, the rooms are simple but comfortable and charming. Meals are prepared from Shaker recipes and served at the Trustee's House, where the leaders of the village once conducted the necessary business with the outside world. A few days at Shaker Village is a serene experience in a hectic world.

Address: 3501 Lexington Rd., Harrodsburg, KY 40330; tel: 606-734-5411.

Accommodations: Eighty-one guest rooms, including some suites, in historic buildings and small houses, all with private baths.

Amenities: Air-conditioning, off-street parking, lectures, exhibitions of Shaker crafts, tours, shops, riverboat excursions from April through October. Dining room for lunch and dinner.

Rates: $$. Visa, MasterCard, personal checks, and cash.

Restrictions: No pets, restricted smoking.

DELAWARE

Armitage Inn

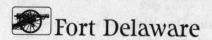 # Fort Delaware

Delaware City, Delaware

Fort Delaware was constructed on Pea Patch Island in the Delaware River to be part of a mid–nineteenth-century coastal defense network of forts. In 1861 the War Department determined that it would be an ideal site for political prisoners, and Confederate officers and enlisted men.

Often as many as 12,500 prisoners were in residence, many living in wooden barracks outside the fort walls. Although the fort was surrounded by a moat, a number of prisoners escaped by swimming to shore, where they were given aid by Southern sympathizers.

The damp, insect-infested terrain fostered epidemics, and some 2,700 prisoners perished. Most of them are buried just across the river in what is now a national cemetery. A museum in the fort houses scale models of the fort and Civil War relics.

The **Delafort,** an 88-passenger ferryboat, takes visitors to the fort from the last weekend in April to the last weekend in September, Saturdays, Sundays, and holidays, 10:00–6:00. It also runs from mid-June to Labor Day, Wednesday, Thursday, and Friday, 10:00–6:00. The ride costs $6 for adults, $4 for children two to twelve. For information phone 302-834-7941.

Armitage Inn

New Castle, Delaware

Built in 1732, the Armitage Inn is beautifully situated on the banks of the river in New Castle's Battery Park, a few steps away from the spot where William Penn first set foot in the New World.

From the steps of this historic inn, you can see Fort Delaware on Pea Patch Island in the Delaware River, where upward of 33,000 Confederates were imprisoned.

There are five handsomely decorated guest rooms, three on the second floor, two on the third. All are sumptuously decorated, and those in the rear have a view of the river. On the ground floor, guests may relax in the parlor, the library, or on a screened porch overlooking a walled garden.

Address: 2 The Strand, New Castle, DE 19720;
  tel: 302-328-6618; fax: 302-324-1163.
Accommodations: Five guest rooms, all with private baths,
  three with whirlpool tubs.
Amenities: Air-conditioning, off-street parking; rooms have
  phones, cable TV, feather beds. Restaurants and antiques
  shops in walking distance.
Rates: $$$. All major credit cards and personal checks.
Restrictions: No children under twelve, no pets, no smoking.

WASHINGTON, DC

Morrison-Clark Inn

*Willard
Inter-Continental*

Willard Inter-Continental

Washington, DC

The Willard isn't what comes to mind when someone says historic inn. The grande dame of Washington now is a luxury hotel offering guests every amenity, but at heart she is one of the great historic inns, albeit one that is twelve stories high and has grown and prospered with the times.

Abraham Lincoln, his family, and several aides stayed here before his inaugural, and his bill for $773.75 is on display in the lobby today. Indeed, every president from Franklin Pierce to Bill Clinton has stayed here on the eve of his nomination. Throughout the war, the Willard was the center for Union generals (Grant stayed here four times) and politicians; in fact, the word "lobbyist" was coined to describe the office-seekers who hung around the Willard lobby hoping to button-hole influential politicians. Julia Ward Howe was a guest here when she wrote the words to "Battle Hymn of the Republic."

While covering the war for *The Atlantic Monthly*, Nathaniel Hawthorne described the Willard: "This hotel, in fact, may be much more justly called the center of Washington and the Union than either the Capitol, the White House or the State Department . . . you exchange nods with governors of sovereign states; you elbow illustrious men, and tread on the toes of generals; you hear statesmen and orators speaking in their familiar tones. You are mixed up with office seekers, wire pullers, inventors, artists, poets, prosers . . . until identity is lost among them."

Address: 1401 Pennsylvania Ave. NW, 20004, two blocks east of the White House; tel: 202-628-9100; fax: 202-637-7326.

Accommodations: 340 first-class rooms, including thirty-eight suites.

Amenities: All rooms are furnished in Queen Anne style. Oversized bathroom with a phone, hair dryer, and television speaker. Concierge. Restaurants include the elegant Willard Room. Shopping. Exercise room. Famous Peacock Alley runs the length of the hotel, connecting Pennsylvania Avenue and F Street.

Rates: $$$. All credit cards accepted.
Restrictions: Some restrictions on pets.

Morrison-Clark Inn

Washington, DC

In 1864 two of Washington's leading families built homes side by side, just northwest of fashionable Massachusetts Avenue, near Mount Vernon Square. Today, these Victorian houses are the heart of a distinctive historic inn. Daniel L. Morrison made a fortune selling flour and feed to the government during the war; Reuben B. Clark, Washington's jail commissioner, became wealthy through land investments. The Morrison house was purchased in 1923 by the Women's Army and Navy League and converted into an inexpensive place for enlisted men to stay while visiting Washington. Later the facility was expanded to include the Clark home. Traditionally, first ladies presided over the club. When it opened in 1923, Grace Coolidge headed the receiving line.

In 1987 the property became the Morrison-Clark Inn after being renovated by William Adair, who supervised the renovation of the White House. He preserved the historic exterior and many of the interior details, including four pier mirrors and Carrara marble fireplaces. Many of the guest rooms contain historic features, and are decorated with period furnishings and original art. The handsome Morrison-Clark Restaurant, one of the finest in the capital area, was cited by *Gourmet* magazine in 1997 as one of "our readers' top tables."

The Morrison-Clark house magically transports guests back in time to a luxurious mansion in Lincoln's Washington.

Address: Massachusetts Ave. and 11th St., NW, Washington, DC 20001; tel: 202-898-1200 or 800-332-7898 (reservations); fax: 202-289-8576.

Accommodations: Fifty-four rooms and suites.

Amenities: Gourmet restaurant (202-289-8580), period furnishings, minibar, hair dryer, voice-mail, twice-daily maid service and nightly turndown, complimentary newspaper, fitness center, parking garage under building.

Rates: $$–$$$. All credit cards and personal checks.

Restrictions: No pets.

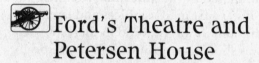

Ford's Theatre and Petersen House

Washington, DC

On the evening of April 14, 1865, John Wilkes Booth, a well-known actor and Southern sympathizer, slipped into the presidential box at Ford's Theatre and shot President Abraham Lincoln in the back of the head. Lincoln, unconscious, was carried across the street and placed on a bed in the Petersen house, where he died the next morning.

Leaping from the box to the stage, Booth broke his leg but managed to hobble out of the theater, mount his horse, and flee the city. Booth was shot to death in a barn at Port Royal, Virginia, on April 26.

The theater was purchased by the government shortly after the assassination. It was first used as offices and later as the Army Medical Museum. It was restored in the 1960s. Box 7, where Lincoln was shot, has reproductions of the original furniture, including the president's rocking chair, in which he sat on the fateful night.

The Petersen house belonged to a German immigrant, William Petersen, a tailor who ran it as a boardinghouse. The ground-floor bedroom where Lincoln died has been restored along with the front parlor where Mrs. Lincoln waited through the night, and the back parlor where Secretary of War Edwin Stanton interviewed witnesses to the shooting. The government purchased the house in 1896.

Ford's Theatre and the Petersen House National Historic Site, 511 and 516 10th St., NW, Washington DC 20002, are open daily, 9:00–5:00, except Christmas. A museum in the theater contains the murder weapon, the flag that covered Lincoln's coffin, the clothing he wore the night he was shot, and other memorabilia connected with the assassination. For information phone 202-426-6924.

In Maryland, some fifteen miles south of Washington on U.S. 31, are two sites connected with Booth's flight from Washington.

Surratt House and Tavern, 9118 Brandywine Rd., Clinton, MD 20735 (once named Surrattsville). John Surratt, one of John Wilkes Booth's co-conspirators, hid weapons in this tavern and post office operated by his mother, Mary. Although

she allegedly had no knowledge of the murder plot, a military court found her guilty of aiding the conspirators, and she was hanged. The jury failed to agree on the guilt of her son, and the charges against him were dropped. Booth stopped here briefly on his flight from Washington, to retrieve a weapon he had hidden here. Open March through December 11, Thursday–Friday, 11:00–3:00, and Saturday–Sunday, 12:00–4:00. Admission is $1.50 for adults, $1 for seniors, and $.50 for children five to eighteen. For information phone 301-868-1121.

Dr. Samuel A. Mudd Home and Museum, just off Poplar Hill Rd. in Waldorf, MD, is the home and plantation of the doctor who set Booth's leg. Dr. Mudd was sent to Fort Jefferson Prison on Dry Tortugas Island, Florida, but was pardoned by President Andrew Johnson in 1869. Open April through November, Wednesday, 11:00–3:00, and Saturday–Sunday, 12:00–4:00. For information phone 301-645-6870.

MARYLAND

Inn at Antietam

Piper House

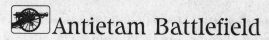# Antietam Battlefield
Sharpsburg, Maryland

On September 17, 1862, the bloodiest day in American history, more than 23,000 men were killed or wounded here as the Army of the Potomac, commanded by General George McClellan, turned back General Robert E. Lee's first invasion of the North.

A Union soldier had stumbled on Lee's tactical plan wrapped around some cigars. Knowing what to expect, McClellan moved cautiously. But by not committing his reserves, he lost the opportunity to crush Lee's Army of Northern Virginia.

The battle, critical because a Confederate victory probably would have brought British aid to the Confederacy, was a tactical draw but a strategic victory for the North, allowing Lincoln to issue the Emancipation Proclamation. Lee withdrew the day after the battle, McClellan did not pursue, and he was soon relieved of command by Lincoln.

Antietam National Battlefield is north and east of Sharpsburg, along MD 34 and 65, both of which routes intersect either U.S. 40 or 40A and I-70. A museum in the **Visitor Center** contains battle artifacts and shows an audiovisual orientation program hourly. Musket and cannon demonstrations and historical talks are given regularly in the summer. Open daily, 9:00–5:00, and 8:30–6:00 in the summer. Closed Thanksgiving, Christmas, and New Year's Day. Admission is $2 for adults, children under seventeen free. For information phone 301-432-5124.

Although **Antietam** is in Maryland, **Gettysburg** in Pennsylvania, and **Harpers Ferry** in West Virginia, they are quite close to one another and all three can be seen on a long weekend. Antietam is ninety minutes southwest of Gettysburg; Harpers Ferry is only thirty minutes south of Antietam. The information desks at each will direct you to the others.

⬛Piper House
Sharpsburg, Maryland

On the morning of the Battle of Antietam, much of the action took place in the cornfield of the Piper Farm. In the afternoon, there was savage fighting at the nearby Bloody Lane. James Longstreet, the general Lee called his "Old War Horse," briefly used this 1840 simple log-and-frame farmhouse as his battlefield headquarters. After the battle, the house and barn were pressed into service as a field hospital that treated both Confederate and Federal wounded. The Piper House, on the national battlefield, is popular with people who want to explore the scene of the bloodiest single day in the war; practically all the important sites are within walking distance.

Innkeepers Louis and Regina Clark, who lease the property from the Park Service, enjoy telling guests the farm's interesting history. The house is decorated in period antiques. The Piper House is one mile north of the town of Sharpsburg on Rte. 65, just before the **Visitor Center** at the battlefield.

Address: PO Box 100, Sharpsburg, MD 21782;
  tel: 301-797-1862.
Accommodations: Three double rooms, all with private baths.
Amenities: Air-conditioning, parking, easy walk to Visitor
  Center.
Rates: $$, including full breakfast. Visa, MasterCard, and personal checks.
Restrictions: No children under ten, no pets, restricted
  smoking.

🏛 Inn at Antietam

Sharpsburg, Maryland

From the front porch of this Victorian farmhouse trimmed with gingerbread, you look across the road and field to Bloody Lane. To the right of the house is the National Cemetery, and you can walk down the road to Burnside's Bridge.

The fighting that went on here is in sharp contrast to the charm and comfort the house offers. The house has been carefully restored in the style of the Civil War period by innkeepers Cal and Betty Fairbourn.

The living room has walnut rococo revival furniture, and guest rooms have Eastlake dressers. One guest room, in the smokehouse behind the main building, has a paneled sitting room with a fireplace and a loft bed. The master suite has a massive antique four-poster bed.

A full breakfast is served on Royal Copenhagen china in the formal dining room. A portrait of General Lee hangs just

outside the dining room and lithographs of the Battle of
Antietam hang in the hall.

Address: 220 E. Main St., PO Box 119, Sharpsburg, MD 21782;
  tel: 301-432-6601; fax: 301-432-5981.
Accommodations: Four suites, all with private baths.
Amenities: Air-conditioning, off-street parking, biking.
Rates: $$. American Express and personal checks.
Restrictions: No children under six, no pets, no smoking.

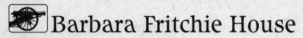

Barbara Fritchie House

Frederick, Maryland

Barbara Fritchie was a ninety-five-year-old widow when she
stood at the gate of her house waving a Union flag as
Stonewall Jackson's troops marched by in September 1862.
When told to put the flag away, she said, "Shoot, if you must,
this old gray head, but spare your country's flag." In John
Greenleaf Whittier's famous poem, Jackson told his troops:
"Who touches a hair on yon gray head dies like a dog!
March on!"

Churchill and Roosevelt visited the house during World
War II, and Churchill, a student of the Civil War, proudly
recited the entire poem from memory.

Damaged by a flood, the original Fritchie house was torn
down in 1927. The replica, built in 1927, displays some of Ms.
Fritchie's furniture and personal possessions.

The **Barbara Fritchie House and Museum,** 154 W. Patrick
St., Frederick, MD 21701, is open April through September,
Monday and Wednesday–Saturday, 10:00–4:00, and Sunday,
1:00–4:00. Docent tours. Gift shop. Admission is $2 for adults,
$1.50 for seniors and children under twelve. For information
phone 301-698-0630.

Monocacy Battlefield

Frederick, Maryland

Confederate general Jubal Early, boldly bound for the virtually defenseless Washington, DC, was met here on July 9, 1864, by green troops commanded by General Lew Wallace. Early won the battle, but it cost him a day and gave reinforcements time to arrive at Washington's defenses. Early was thrown back at Fort Stevens in the District of Columbia, and retreated to Virginia, ending the last Confederate attempt to carry the war to the North. At the battlefield a monument is inscribed with Wallace's words: "These men died to save the National Capital, and they did save it."

Monocacy National Battlefield, 4801 Urbana Pike, Frederick, MD 21704, is open from Memorial Day–Labor Day, seven days a week, 8:00–4:30; the rest of the year Wednesday–Sunday. Admission is free. The **Visitor Center** contains artifacts of the battle. To reach the battlefield from Frederick, take MD 355 south, and just beyond the railroad overpass, turn left. A stone mill marks the site of the battle. For information phone 301-662-3515.

Spring Bank Inn

Frederick, Maryland

A Rhode Island regiment, on its way from Sharpsburg, encamped where this 1880 brick farmhouse now stands, two and a half miles north of the center of Frederick, and an easy drive from the Monocacy battlefield.

The restored house is an attractive blend of Gothic revival and Italianate features—etched glass on the front door, faux-marble mantels, William Morris wallpaper, random-width floors, a fresco on the ceiling of one of the guest rooms.

Ray and Beverly Compton, the owners and hosts, were honored by the Historical Society of Frederick for restoring the house to its past glory. Porches shade three sides of the house and there are ten acres of farmland to the rear.

Frederick is known for the quantity and quality of its antique shops. Beverly knows who sells what and where to go for the "good stuff," and will share her expertise with guests.

Address: 7945 Worman's Mill Rd., Frederick, MD 21701; tel: 301-694-0440; E-mail: rcomp1880@aol.com.

Accommodations: One double with private bath, four doubles share two and a half baths.

Amenities: Air-conditioning, off-street parking, cable TV in parlor.

Rates: $$, including continental breakfast. All major credit cards.

Restrictions: No children under twelve, no pets, no smoking.

PENNSYLVANIA

Beechmont Inn

Cashtown Inn

Doubleday Inn

The Bafferton Inn

Farnsworth House

Baladerry Inn

Beechmont Inn

Hanover, Pennsylvania

This inn, a Georgian town house built in 1834, is near the town square. During the Battle of Gettysburg, fought twenty miles to the west, some of the fighting splashed over into this town.

General H. Judson Kilpatrick clashed here with Jeb Stuart, Lee's cavalry leader, and was forced to retreat down the street in front of the house. He passed by again when George Armstrong Custer forced the Confederates back through the center of town.

The fighting here prevented Stuart from arriving at Gettysburg until the second day of the battle, a delay that kept Lee from receiving a report on the strength and location of Union forces. Many historians believe this was an important factor in the Union victory.

Owners William and Susan Day are proud of their inn, furnished with antiques from the Federal period and with upstairs guest rooms named after Civil War generals. A downstairs suite has a private entrance onto the inn's garden courtyard, which is shaded by a century-old magnolia tree. A gourmet breakfast is a highlight of a stay at Beechmont, and specialties include apple-baked French toast and a California egg puff.

Address: 315 Broadway, Hanover, PA 17331; tel: 717-632-3013.
Accommodations: Four double rooms and three suites, all with private baths, one with whirlpool and some with fireplaces.
Amenities: Fishing, riding, swimming, and boating in nearby state park, three public golf courses, antiques shops.
Rates: $$. All major credit cards, personal checks, and cash.
Restrictions: No children under twelve, no pets, no smoking.

Cashtown Inn

Cashtown, Pennsylvania

Before and after the Battle of Gettysburg, the Army of Northern Virginia passed through this crossroads village. General A. P. Hill made his headquarters at the 1797 inn, and it was here that he gave General Henry Heth permission to take troops into Gettysburg to look for a rumored supply of shoes.

Early in the afternoon of July 1, 1863, Lee stopped by the inn to see Hill as he made his way toward the sound of the guns. More recently, actor Sam Elliott (who played Union general John Buford) made his headquarters here during the filming of the movie *Gettysburg*.

Also in residence here is a ghost. Sightings have been reported of a Confederate soldier in slouch hat and tattered uniform. He occasionally startles guests staying in Room 4, and he is blamed for unexplained rapping at the door of the room.

Ghost or no, Dennis and Eileen Hoover run a good inn: the rooms are comfortable, there is a tavern, the food in the dining room is good, and some interesting Civil War art and photographs hang on the walls downstairs. Cashtown is eight miles west of Gettysburg.

Address: PO Box 103, 1325 Old Rte. 30, Cashtown, PA 17310; tel: 800-367-1797 or 717-334-9722; fax: 717-334-1442.

Accommodations: Five guest rooms and two family suites, all with private baths.

Amenities: Air-conditioning, off-street parking, full-service restaurant.

Rates: $$–$$$. American Express, Visa, MasterCard, Discover, and personal checks.

Restrictions: Children allowed only in family suites, no pets, restricted smoking.

Gettysburg Battlefield

Gettysburg, Pennsylvania

In June 1863, Lee marched his army north through Maryland and into Pennsylvania in the hope that a major victory on Northern soil would compel the Union to sue for peace. He was pursued by George Meade, recently appointed commander of the Army of the Potomac. They met by chance at Gettysburg.

A rumor spread that a warehouse in Gettysburg was full of shoes, which the rebels badly needed. A small force rode off to investigate and ran smack into a Federal patrol, and that chance encounter escalated into one of the greatest battles ever fought in the Western Hemisphere.

On the first day, July 1, the rebels struck Federal troops at McPherson Ridge, just west of town. The outnumbered Federals were driven back to a position on Cemetery Ridge, south of town.

On the second day, Lee took up a position on Seminary Ridge, parallel to the Union position on Cemetery Ridge, and ordered an attack against both Union flanks. General James Longstreet hit the left at Little Round Top, leaving Union dead on the Wheat Field and overrunning the Peach Orchard. In the evening, General Richard Ewell struck the Union right at East Cemetery Hill and Culp's Hill. None of the three attacks was able to dislodge Meade from Cemetery Ridge.

On the fateful third day, Lee, over Longstreet's objections, ordered an all-out assault aimed right at the center of the Union line. His artillery began a bombardment of Cemetery Ridge, touching off a two-hour artillery duel. In the afternoon, Lee sent some thirteen thousand men across the mile of open field toward the "little clump of trees" that marked the Union center. The attack, known as Pickett's Charge, never really had a chance. A handful of rebels breached the Union lines, but to no avail. Only one in three Confederates survived the charge.

The next day, July 4, the remains of Lee's army headed for the Potomac and home. Its losses were irreplaceable, and Lee could never again launch a major offensive. A lot of fighting lay ahead, but although no one realized it, the Confederacy had lost the war.

Gettysburg National Military Park, 97 Taneytown Rd., is open daily, 6:00–10:00; the **Visitor Center,** 8:00–5:00. Admission to the park is free. Most visitors take a self-guided tour through the park's approximately five thousand acres and thirty-five miles of roads. An audio cassette offers a mile-by-mile auto tour, and is available in the **Visitor Center** bookstore. For information phone 717-334-1124. A ninety-minute tape and a player may be rented at the **National Civil War Wax Museum,** 297 Steinwehr Ave. For information phone 717-334-6245.

Another way to see the area is to engage a Battlefield Guide, licensed by the Park Service, to accompany you in your car (or drive your car, if you wish). Later this year, reservations for guided tours will be available. The cost for a two-hour tour with up to five people in the car is $30.

The **Visitor Center** contains the "electric map" that shows troop movement during the battle, a museum, and bookstore. From mid-June to September there are ranger-guided walks. Admission to the map is $3 for adults, $2.50 for seniors, and $1.50 for children sixteen and under.

The **National Cemetery,** where Lincoln delivered his Gettysburg Address, is across the street from the **Visitor Center**. A battle seminar is held in March. For information phone 717-334-0772.

Across the parking lot to the right of the **Visitor Center** is the **Cyclorama Center,** where exhibits include a short film, *From These Honored Dead,* and the 356-foot-long painting of Pickett's Charge, displayed in a special program with a sound-and-light show. Admission is $3 for adults, $2.50 for seniors, and $1.50 for children sixteen and under.

IN THE FOOTSTEPS OF PICKETT'S BRAVE MEN

To sense what it must have been like to be part of Pickett's Charge, go to the Lee statue on Seminary Ridge, and look up and see the "little clump of trees" a mile away on Seminary Ridge that marked the center of the Union line. Imagine this is July 3, 1863. It is early afternoon and it is very hot.

You are one of thirteen thousand Confederate soldiers waiting for the signal to charge. You are carrying a rifle and about twenty pounds of ammunition and equipment, and you are frightened.

The signal comes, and you are running across the field and up the gentle hill, the eerie sound of rebel yells ringing in your ears. Officers on horseback waving swords urge you on.

You're halfway up the hill now, and you're beginning to think you may live through this after all. Suddenly there is a thunderous roar—a hundred cannon and thousands of small arms are firing at you. Your friends are falling on either side of you . . .

At a leisurely pace, the mile walk takes about twenty-five minutes. It is a memorable experience, particularly for teenagers.

A WALKING TOUR OF THE TOWN

An excellent way to see the historic sights is to take a self-guided walking tour of Gettysburg. At the **Western Maryland Railroad Passenger Depot,** 35 Carlisle St., is the **Gettysburg Convention and Visitors Bureau,** where you can pick up a free tour map. The exterior of the depot looks the same today as it did when President Lincoln arrived in November 1863 to dedicate the cemetery. The **Gettysburg Convention and Visitors Bureau** (35 Carlisle St., Gettysburg, PA 17325) provides information about the area. For information phone 717-334-6274.

The walking tour passes thirty-five points of interest and should take about two hours. For information phone 717-334-6274. Another way to see the sights is by renting a horse-drawn carriage. For information phone Dayhoff's Carriages, 717-337-2276.

Gettysburg is the ultimate Civil War treasure trove. There is a great deal to see and do here, and visitors should plan to stay several days. In addition to the sites, the town plays host to a number of special events. **Civil War Heritage Days,** in late June and early July, include a collectors' show, a Civil War book show, fireworks, a parade, and thousands of uniformed enthusiasts in town to reenact the battle.

The **Confederate States Armory and Museum,** 529 Baltimore St., features a collection of rare Confederate small arms, edged weapons, and memorabilia. Usually open daily except Tuesday, 12:00–5:00. Admission is $2, $1.50 for children. For information phone 717-337-2340.

Jenny Wade House Museum, 548 Baltimore St. The 1863 home of the only civilian casualty of the battle (see **Farnsworth House,** page 53) has its original furnishings. Open daily, 9:00–5:00, except December through February. Admission is $5.25 for adults, $4.75 for seniors, and $3.25 for children. For information phone 717-334-4100.

Lincoln Room Museum, 12 Lincoln Square, is located in the historic Wills House, where Lincoln stayed the night before he delivered his Gettysburg Address on November 19, 1863. The house had been used as a hospital after the battle. The room where Lincoln slept has its original furnishings. An audiovisual program is provided. Usually open daily, 9:00–5:00. Admission is $3.25 for adults, $3 for seniors, and $1.75 for children.

Events are scheduled in Gettysburg every year for the anniversary of Lincoln's Address, November 19. On Remembrance Day, the Saturday closest to November 19, a parade is held, sponsored by the Sons of Union Veterans.

General Lee's Headquarters, 401 Buford Ave., is a small stone house used by Lee on the first day of the battle. It contains a small museum that displays artifacts related to the battle. Open daily in the summer, 9:00–9:00, and 9:00–5:00 the rest of the year. Admission is $2 for adults, free for children under twelve.

The Conflict, 213 Steinwehr Ave., is a triple-screen program depicting the Civil War with an emphasis on Gettysburg. Daily, 9:00–5:00 and summer evenings. Admission is $5 for adults, $4 for seniors and students. For information phone 717-334-8003.

Gettysburg Battle Theatre, 571 Steinwehr Ave., has a thirty-minute multimedia program showing the strategy of the battle, employing a miniature battlefield and 25,000 figures. Open March through November, daily, 9:30–7:30. Admission is $5.25 for adults, $4.75 for seniors, and $3.25 for children eight to eleven. For information phone 717-334-6100.

National Tower, one mile south via U.S. 97, has four observation decks on a 300-foot-high tower permitting a 360-degree view of the battlefield. A short audiovisual program prepares visitors for what they will see from the tower. Open April through October, 9:00–6:30; weekends only the rest of the year; call ahead during winter. Admission is $5 for adults, $4.50 for seniors, and $3 for children. For information phone 717-334-6754.

Lincoln Train Museum, a half-mile south via U.S. 15 on Steinwehr Ave. Visitors can take a simulated Lincoln Train Ride of twenty miles while a guide explains why and how the president came to Gettysburg. The museum features more than one thousand model trains and railroad memorabilia. Usually open daily, 9:00–8:30. Admission is $5.25 for adults, $4.50 for seniors, and $3.25 for children. For information phone 717-334-5678.

Doubleday Inn

Gettysburg, Pennsylvania

On July 1, the first day of the battle, a Confederate force was met by General Abner Doubleday's division at Oak Ridge, just across the road from this inn. The fighting raged until Jubal Early's rebels drove the Union troops back toward Gettysburg, a mile to the southeast. Some of the Confederate dead were buried in Iverson's Pit, a few hundred yards from here.

Although not built until 1929, the inn is actually on the battlefield. It was named after Doubleday (spuriously credited with inventing baseball), who held off the rebels long enough for reinforcements to arrive.

The inn is big, handsome, and comfortable, decorated in a mixture of "Americana and English country." The bedrooms are stenciled, colorful quilts cover the beds, and Union and Confederate flags are painted near the front door.

On Wednesday and Saturday nights during the summer, a historian comes to the inn to lead discussions about various aspects of the battle. And from time to time, "Lieutenant Marcellus Jones," who says he fired the first shot of the battle, rides up to the delight of both adults and children, who are allowed to sit on his horse.

Address: 104 Doubleday Ave., Gettysburg, PA 17325; tel: 717-334-9119.

Accommodations: Nine guest rooms, five with private baths.

Amenities: Air-conditioning, off-street parking, afternoon refreshments, historical discussions, bicycling.

Rates: $$, including an afternoon tea. Visa, MasterCard, Discover, and personal checks.

Restrictions: No children under seven, no smoking.

The Bafferton Inn

Gettysburg, Pennsylvania

During the first day of battle, as retreating Union troops swept by this house, a stray shot shattered an upstairs window, the bullet lodging in the fireplace mantel where it remains today. Later, when the nearby Catholic church was being used as a hospital, masses were held in what is now the living room.

Now a charming inn, the house is a half-block from Lincoln Square and the Wills House, where Lincoln put the finishing touches on his Gettysburg Address. The inn, listed on the National Register of Historic Places, was built in 1786, and was the first house in what became the town of Gettysburg.

Sam and Jane Back own and operate the inn. They were

educators in a New England prep school until they decided they "wanted to do something different." They have furnished the inn with eighteenth- and nineteenth-century antiques, and graced the walls with elaborate stencils and family portraits. A folk art mural encircles the living room.

In January, the inn, in conjunction with several other local inns, hosts a Civil War ball, and many guests come dressed in uniforms and period clothing. On other winter weekends, guests dine with Lincoln (portrayed by a local actor) and listen to a concert of Civil War band music.

Address: 44 York St., Gettysburg, PA 17325; tel: 717-337-3423.
Accommodations: Eight double rooms and two suites, all with private baths.
Amenities: Air-conditioning, off-street parking.
Rates: $$. American Express, Visa, MasterCard, Discover, and personal checks.
Restrictions: No children under eight, no pets, no smoking.

Baladerry Inn
Gettysburg, Pennsylvania

During the battle, this peaceful refuge was a madhouse. Two miles down Blacksmith Shop Road there was fierce fighting at Little Round Top and Devil's Den. A bit north was the Wheat Field, where more than six thousand men fell. Three miles up Baltimore Pike was the Union line on Cemetery Ridge, the objective of General Pickett.

This old stone and brick house, built in 1812 as part of Spangler's Farm, was used as a field hospital, and Confederate general Lewis Armistead, who was mortally wounded leading Pickett's Charge, died on the Farm.

Today, an addition and a carriage house complement the original structure. The guest rooms and common areas have been tastefully furnished with antiques and reproductions. The innkeepers, Tom and Caryl O'Gara, who radiate Irish hospitality, named the inn after the town in Ireland where Tom's ancestors lived.

Address: 40 Hospital Rd., Gettysburg, PA 17325; tel: 717-337-1342.
Accommodations: Two double rooms in the original house, six more in the carriage house, all with private baths.
Amenities: Air-conditioning, off-street parking, cable TV in the common rooms of both buildings, tennis court, game room, bicycling, picnic baskets on request.
Rates: $$, including informal afternoon tea. All major credit cards and personal checks.
Restrictions: No children under fourteen, no pets, restricted smoking.

Farnsworth House
Gettysburg, Pennsylvania

The one civilian killed in the Battle of Gettysburg was Jenny Wade, struck by a stray bullet while working in her kitchen. Her house, now a museum, is just down the street from the inn. The shot, experts believe, came from one of the Confederate sharpshooters firing from the garret of this house. Some 150 bullets struck this house as Union troops attempted to silence the sharpshooters.

Today, many people believe that Jenny Wade is one of the ghosts still haunting this inn. Patti O'Day, the daughter of innkeeper Loring Shultz, conducts a ghost tour of the house, and has discussed the ghosts of Gettysburg on national television.

Gettysburg is believed to be the most haunted place in the country. The 51,000 casualties here, they say, produced a lot of restless spirits. Should you hear moans in the night, just pull the covers over your head and try to go back to sleep.

Ghosts or no, this is a comfortable old inn filled with artifacts, many of them dug from the nearby battlefield. The attic contains display cases of grenades, artillery shells, and bullets.

The cozy guest rooms are furnished with period antiques. On the walls of the candlelit dining room are portraits of Lee and Meade and photographs by Matthew Brady. If you dine here, you may order such Civil War-era fare as peanut soup, pumpkin fritters, and sweet potato pudding.

Address: 401 Baltimore St., Gettysburg, PA 17325;
 tel: 717-334-8838; fax: 717-334-5862.
Accommodations: Five guest rooms, all with private baths.
Amenities: Air-conditioning, off-street parking, TV in sitting
 room, restaurant, house tour, antique shop, concierge,
 bellman.
Rates: $$. American Express, Visa, MasterCard, and Discover.
Restrictions: No pets, no smoking in guest rooms.

Gettystown Inn and Dobbin House Tavern

Gettysburg, Pennsylvania

The Dobbin House had been in existence for some time when Lincoln passed by on his way to dedicate the new national cemetery just down the street. In fact, it's the oldest building in the area. Built in 1776 and now on the National Register, the house was the Dobbin family's private residence. In the 1850s it was a station on the Underground Railroad. Fugitive slaves were hidden in a space that can still be seen next to the walk-in fireplace. During the battle, the Dobbin House was used as a hospital.

The Dobbin House Tavern offers both a continental menu and dishes of the Civil War period. (Open daily, 5:00–10:00, except Thanksgiving, Christmas, and New Year's Day. Lunch served daily in Springhouse Tavern, opening at 11:30. Reservations: 717-334-2100. Same credit cards as Inn.)

Next door is the Gettystown Inn, a Civil War-era house beautifully restored and furnished with period antiques. The guest rooms are named after generals who fought here—Lee, Pickett, Steinwehr, Stuart, and Reynolds. In the common room is cable TV, a VCR, and a selection of tapes of Civil War movies. Guests are served breakfast at the Dobbin House.

Address: 89 Steinwehr Ave., Gettysburg, PA 17325; tel: 717-334-2100; fax: 717-334-6905; E-mail: inn@dobbinhouse.com.

Accommodations: Five double rooms, all with private baths.

Amenities: Air-conditioning, off-street parking, restaurant, cable TV with VCR in common room.

Rates: $$. American Express, Visa, and MasterCard.

Restrictions: No pets, no smoking.

WEST VIRGINIA

*Fillmore Street
Bed and Breakfast*

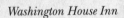

Washington House Inn

The Carriage Inn

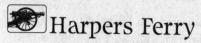 # Harpers Ferry
West Virginia

John Brown, a militant abolitionist, slipped into town here on the evening of October 16, 1859, planning to capture the armory and distribute weapons to the slaves who, he believed, would rise in rebellion. His twenty-two-man "army of liberation" took control of the armory but, finding themselves outnumbered, took several hostages and barricaded themselves in the fire house.

Troops brought from Washington by Robert E. Lee stormed the building and took Brown prisoner. Ten of Brown's men, including two of his sons, were among those killed. Brought to trial for murder, treason, and conspiring with slaves to create insurrection, Brown was found guilty, and hanged at nearby Charles Town.

During the war, the town became the base of operations

for Union invasions into the Shenandoah Valley. Stonewall Jackson achieved his most brilliant victory here in 1862, when he captured 12,500 Federal soldiers.

Harpers Ferry National Historical Park is open daily except Christmas, 8:00–5:00, although not much happens here in the winter. Admission is $5 for cars, $3 for walk-ins. The election of 1860 is re-created the second full weekend in October. From Washington take I-270 north to I-70 to Rte. 340; from Gettysburg take MD 15 south to Rte. 340 west; from Baltimore take I-70 west to Rte. 340 west. For further information phone 304-535-6029 for the **Information Center,** or 304-535-6298 for the **Visitor Center** (PO Box 65, Harpers Ferry, WV 25425). Across the river from Harpers Ferry, in Maryland, is the **Kennedy Farm,** an innocent-looking farmhouse, now a National Historic Landmark, that was the staging area where John Brown and his followers planned and prepared for their Harpers Ferry raid during the summer of

1859. Open May through October, Saturday and Sunday, 9:00–5:00. Admission is free. The grounds are open all year. The **Kennedy Farm** is at 2406 Chestnut Grove Rd., Sharpsburg, MD 21782. From I-70 take exit 29 to Rte. 65 south for about ten miles. For information phone 301-645-6870.

Fillmore Street Bed and Breakfast

Harpers Ferry, West Virginia

A visitor might well think that the national historic park contains all of Harpers Ferry, but there is more to the town at the top of the hill. There lies the Fillmore Street Bed and Breakfast, a Victorian cottage that dates from 1890, but is built on the foundation of a Civil War-era house. When Stonewall Jackson swooped down on the town in 1862, there was fighting on and around the property.

Today guests enjoy the garden rocking chairs on the front porch and the view of the mountains. Good reading awaits in the little library between the guest rooms. The house is a charmer, with blue-green shutters and a white picket fence. When you've explored the rest of Harpers Ferry, hosts James and Alden Addy will direct you to some of the other pleasures of the area—river sports, biking, antiquing, and exploring the old C & O Canal towpath.

Address: 630 Fillmore St. (PO Box 34), Harpers Ferry, WV 25425; tel: 304-535-2619.
Accommodations: Two double rooms, both with private baths.
Amenities: Air-conditioning, fireplaces, in-room TV, afternoon tea or sherry.
Rates: $$, including either full breakfast at 9:00 or continental breakfast in room. Personal checks or cash only.
Restrictions: No children under twelve, no pets, no smoking.

Jefferson County Courthouse
Charles Town, West Virginia

Ten days after his raid on Harpers Ferry, the trial of John
Brown began in Charles Town. The injured Brown was car-
ried into the courthouse and lay on a cot throughout the trial.
The trial lasted a week; the jury deliberated forty-five minutes.
Brown showed no emotion when he was sentenced to

hang. On his way to his execution, he handed a guard a note that read: "I, John Brown, am now quite certain that the crimes of this guilty land will never be purged away but with blood."

The 1836 courthouse, located at the corner of North George and East Washington Sts., was shelled during the war and rebuilt, but the courtroom used during Brown's trial survived intact. Open weekdays. Guided tours on weekend afternoons. For information phone 304-725-9761.

The **Jefferson County Museum,** North Samuel and East Washington Sts., houses Brown memorabilia, including the wagon that transported him to his execution. Open April through November, daily except Sunday, 10:00–4:00. Admission is free. For information phone 304-725-8628. Hours vary. Phone first.

The Carriage Inn

Charles Town, West Virginia

On September 17, 1864, Ulysses S. Grant and Philip Sheridan met in this house to plan Sheridan's devastating Valley Campaign. Neither the generals nor their aides suspected that hidden beneath the hearth in the Rose Room was the flag of Stonewall Jackson's Corps, which had been commissioned by Thomas Rutherford, the owner of the house. The flag now hangs in the Virginia Military Institute museum.

The 1836 house now is an inn owned and operated by Al and Kay Standish. It is three blocks from the courthouse where abolitionist John Brown was tried, and a similar distance from where he was hanged. Civil War mementos and books are in the West Parlor, and guests breakfast in the East Parlor, where the Yankee generals met.

Address: 417 East Washington St., Charles Town, WV 25414; tel: 304-728-8003 or 800-867-9830; E-mail: carriage@intrepid.net.
Accommodations: Six bedrooms with queen-size beds, all with private baths.

Amenities: Air-conditioning, off-street parking; five of the
bedrooms have working fireplaces. TV in common room.
Rates: $$–$$$. Visa, MasterCard, and personal checks.
Restrictions: No children under ten, no pets, restricted smoking.

Washington House Inn

Charles Town, West Virginia

Near the courthouse where John Brown stood trial for his
raid on Harpers Ferry is a stately Queen Anne Victorian,
built at the turn of the century by descendants of George
Washington's brothers, John Augustine and Samuel. George
Washington had surveyed the area earlier, and the town was
named after another brother, Charles.

The inn has seven fireplaces with carved oak mantels, and
is furnished with antiques and period reproductions.
Innkeepers Mel and Nina Vogel will help you plan your stay in
Charles Town. The sites within walking distance include the
Jefferson County Museum, which displays Civil War and John
Brown memorabilia, including the wagon in which he rode to
his death, and the site of the gallows where the abolitionist was
hanged.

Charles Town was a pocket of pro-Confederacy sentiment
when West Virginia voted to leave Virginia and become a state
of its own. The town was heavily shelled during fighting in the
area. Charles Town is a fifteen-minute drive from Harpers Ferry.

Address: 216 South George St., Charles Town, WV 25414;
tel: 304-725-7923 or 800-297-6957.
Accommodations: Six guest rooms, all with full baths.
Amenities: Air-conditioning, off-street parking, TV, coffee and
tea always available, complimentary fresh fruit and cookies.
Rates: $$–$$$. All major credit cards, and personal checks.
Restrictions: No children under ten, no pets, no smoking.

THE SOUTH

VIRGINIA

Edgewood Plantation

Lynchburg Mansion Inn

Inn at Narrow Passage

The Owl and the Pussycat

The Kenmore Inn

The Morrison House

Alexandria, Virginia

Robert E. Lee grew up in this town on the Potomac. He lived with his mother in the Federal-style house at 614 Oronoco St., attended services at Christ Church, 118 Washington St., and his home from his marriage until the war was the Custis Mansion in nearby Arlington. While he shopped in the Stabler Leadbeater Apothecary, 105 South Fairfax St., he received orders to go to Harpers Ferry to put down John Brown's raid.

Alexandria's best inn, the Morrison House, looks as if it were built in colonial days, but actually the five-story Federal-style building was constructed in 1985. The owner then, Robert E. Morrison, had a Smithsonian curator make sure the inn was authentic to the last luxurious detail.

Antiques at the Winterthur Museum in Delaware were models for many of the furnishings, including sofas upholstered in silk brocade, oversized mahogany canopy beds, and gilt-framed mirrors.

The inn has two restaurants: the award-winning Elysium, which features contemporary upscale American cuisine, and the club-like Grill, which has a piano bar.

Address: 116 South Alfred St., Alexandria, VA 22314; tel: 703-838-8000 or 800-367-0800; fax: 703-684-6283.

Accommodations: Forty-five guest rooms, including three suites.

Amenities: Air-conditioning, parking garage for an additional fee, cable TV in rooms, afternoon tea (extra charge), nightly turndown, health club privileges, butler service, easy walk to historic landmarks.

Rates: $$$, including continental breakfast. All major credit cards except Discover.

Restrictions: No pets, restricted smoking.

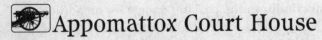Arlington House

Arlington, Virginia

Robert E. Lee loved Arlington House, his mansion on a hill overlooking Washington from across the Potomac. It was built by George Washington Parke Custis, the grandson of Martha Washington by her first marriage, and the father of Mary Anna Randolph Custis, whom Lee married two years after graduating from West Point.

Although the Lees spent much of their married life traveling between army posts, this was home to them for thirty years. Six of their seven children were born here. After Virginia seceded from the Union, it was at Arlington House that Lee made his decision to resign his commission in the U.S. Army rather than bear arms against his native state.

The mansion later became the headquarters of officers supervising the defense of Washington. Later still it was confiscated for back taxes. A two-hundred-acre section of the estate was set aside as an army cemetery, the beginning of Arlington National Cemetery.

Arlington House can be reached from Washington and Alexandria on the Metro trains (Blue Line). Parking is available at the **Arlington Cemetery Visitor Center**. It is open daily, 9:30–4:30. Admission is free. For information phone 703-557-0613.

Appomattox Court House

Appomattox, Virginia

The end of the line for Robert E. Lee and his Army of Northern Virginia came on Palm Sunday 1865, in this sleepy village, ninety-two miles west of Richmond. His surrender to Ulysses S. Grant did not end the war, but it might as

well have. Richmond had fallen, Jefferson Davis and his cabinet were on the run, and William T. Sherman was closing in on Joseph E. Johnston's army.

On April 9, 1865, Lee was waiting in the parlor of the Wilmer McLean house when Grant rode up. They quickly agreed on the terms of the surrender. After the surrender, Union batteries began to fire salutes, but Grant ordered them stopped. "The war is over," he said. "The rebels are our countrymen again."

A formal ceremony was held three days later, during which Lee's men surrendered their arms and battle flags. As they marched by, Joshua Chamberlain, who was accepting the surrender for Grant, ordered his men to present arms. The Confederates returned the salute, a soldier's farewell.

Appomattox Court House is open daily, except Federal

holidays in the winter; June through August, 9:00–5:30; rest of year, 8:30–5:00. Admission is $2 for adults, children under sixteen free. The **national historical park** is on VA 24, three miles northeast of Appomattox. For information phone 804-352-8987.

The Bailiwick Inn

Fairfax, Virginia

In a skirmish fought across the front lawn of this inn, June 1, 1861, Captain John Quincy Marr, commander of the Warrenton Rifles, became the first Confederate casualty of the Civil War in this area. Governor William "Extra-Billy" Smith, who was in the house at the time, took over command from Marr, thus beginning his military career at the age of sixty-four.

The first major battle of the war was fought five miles away at Manassas in 1861. In 1863, the house was searched by John Mosby's Raiders during their midnight raid on Fairfax.

One of the first houses built in Fairfax, the house is in the National Register of Historic Places. The guest rooms, all unique, are furnished with antiques and period reproductions, feather beds, and goose-down pillows, upon which guests will find a chocolate when they turn in.

Innkeepers Bob and Annette Bradley make sure that fresh-cut flowers brighten the foyer, cheery fires burn in fireplaces in book-lined parlors, and silver and crystal grace the breakfast table.

Address: 4023 Chain Bridge Rd., Fairfax, VA 22030; tel: 703-691-2266 or 800-366-7666; fax: 703-934-2112.
Accommodations: Fourteen guest rooms, all named after famous Virginians, all with private baths.
Amenities: Air-conditioning, off-street parking, afternoon tea, candlelight dinner with advance notice (and extra charge), fireplaces.

Rates: $$$. American Express, Visa, MasterCard, and personal checks.
Restrictions: No pets, restricted smoking.

Manassas Battlefield

Manassas, Virginia

The two battles that took place here in 1861 and 1862 are known in the North as First and Second Bull Run, after a creek that runs through the battlefield; in the South they are called First and Second Manassas, after the nearby town.

The 1861 clash was the first major battle of the war, the one in which Thomas J. Jackson won the nickname "Stonewall." The fighting was confused. Troops on both sides were green, and some of the Confederates wore blue and some of the Federals wore gray. Fresh rebel reserves arrived in the late afternoon, and the Federals retreated.

The retreat turned into a rout, but the tired rebels were not able to press their advantage. The victory gave the South a false sense of confidence, and convinced the North that the war would not be won easily. It also cost General Irvin McDowell command of the Union army.

The second battle began August 26, 1862, after Stonewall Jackson's corps reached Union supplies stockpiled at Manassas, took what they could, and retreated a few miles west to a system of ditches that had been dug for a railroad.

General John Pope attacked Jackson, believing the rebels were in retreat. But he found them well entrenched and spoiling for a fight. When Pope's attack stalled, General James Longstreet struck the Union flank with devastating effect. The fighting that day ended at Henry House Hill, where the Federals were able to halt the Confederates.

The next day Pope, having suffered heavy losses, pulled his army back to Washington. Encouraged by the victory, Lee soon embarked on the invasion of Maryland that culminated in the Battle of Antietam.

Manassas National Battlefield Park, 6511 Sudly Rd., Manassas, VA 20109, is open daily except Christmas, dawn to dusk, the **Visitor Center,** 8:30–5:00. Admission is $2 for adults, children under seventeen free. The park, which commemorates both battles, is twenty-six miles southwest of Washington, DC. For information phone 703-361-1339.

Belle Boyd Cottage

Front Royal, Virginia

Belle Boyd was an attractive young lady who spied for Stonewall Jackson, while operating out of her father's hotel in Front Royal. She rode her horse across the field where the Battle of Front Royal was being fought to give Jackson details about the size and disposition of the Federal forces. In gratitude, he made her an honorary captain in his regiment.

Sometime later, betrayed by her lover, she was arrested and held in the Old Capitol Prison in Washington. Exchanged after a month, she went back to spying and was imprisoned again in June 1863. Paroled on her promise to leave the country, she was on a blockade runner that was captured by a Union navy vessel. She and the captain fell in love and were married.

The Belle Boyd Cottage, 101 Chester St., Front Royal, VA 22630, is a typical 1860 middle-class house, furnished in the period. It has been restored as a living history museum depicting Warren County during the war. The guided tour includes interesting stories of Belle and her clandestine activities. Open Monday–Friday, 11:00–4:00, and weekends by appointment. Admission is $2 for adults, $1 for children. On the Saturday nearest May 23, the Battle of Front Royal is reenacted nearby. To reach the cottage follow Rte. 522 (Commerce St.) into Front Royal. For information phone 540-636-1446.

Chester House

Front Royal, Virginia

In the historical district of Front Royal, near the Belle Boyd Cottage, is a stately Georgian mansion, a 1905 updating of a house built in 1848. The house is a treasure, with intricate woodwork, elaborate dentil molding, crystal chandeliers, Oriental rugs, and family antiques and artwork. The attractive bedrooms overlook an Old English garden with brick paths, a fountain, and statuary. A carriage house has a family suite.

Now an inn, the Chester House has been awarded three stars by the *Mobil Guide* and three diamonds by the AAA. A half-block from the inn is the Warren Rifles Confederate Museum, which has a collection of flags, arms, uniforms, relics, and personal memorabilia. On U.S. 522 just north of town is a marker noting where Custer executed several of Mosby's Raiders in 1864. (Two months later, Mosby executed an equal number of Custer's men near Berryville.)

Address: 43 Chester St., Front Royal, VA 22630; tel: 540-635-3937 or 800-621-0441; fax: 540-636-8695; Web page: www.chesterhouse.com.

Accommodations: Six double rooms, four with private baths.

Amenities: Air-conditioning, off-street parking, complimentary refreshments, lawn games.

Rates: $$ (carriage house $$$), including continental breakfast. All major credit cards, and personal checks.

Restrictions: No children under twelve, no pets, restricted smoking.

Fredericksburg Battlefields

Fredericksburg, Virginia

When Lincoln approved Ambrose Burnside's plan to drive to Richmond through Fredericksburg, he cautioned the general, "It will succeed if you move rapidly; otherwise not." Burnside didn't heed Lincoln's warning and met with disaster.

In the **Battle of Fredericksburg (December 13, 1862)** Burnside launched two attacks: one struck the Confederate left at Prospect Hill, the second was aimed at the heart of Lee's defenses on Marye's Heights directly behind Fredericksburg. Union soldiers were slaughtered by artillery on the heights, near the mansion Brompton, and by Confederate infantry firing from behind a stone wall at the foot of the hill. By the end of the day Lee had won his most one-sided victory of the war.

The **Battle of Chancellorsville (May 1–4, 1863)** was another triumph for Lee, this time against General Joseph Hooker. Outnumbered, the defeated Hooker retired across the Rappahannock, and Lee prepared his second invasion of the North. It was during this battle that Stonewall Jackson was mistakenly wounded by his own men; he died eight days later.

The **Battle of the Wilderness (May 5–7, 1864)** was the first encounter between Lee and General Ulysses S. Grant. When the bloody fighting reached a stalemate, Grant elected to go around Lee and march toward Richmond.

Savage fighting started up again two days later in the **Battle of Spotsylvania Court House (May 7–20, 1864),** and again the battle produced no clear-cut victory. Grant sidestepped and moved closer to Richmond. The relentless attrition of these battles and those that followed finally destroyed the offensive capabilities of Lee's Army of Northern Virginia.

The **Fredericksburg and Spotsylvania County Battlefields Memorial National Military Park** is situated on approximately eight thousand acres and includes parts of all four battlefields. There are other important sites well worth visiting: the museum in the **Fredericksburg Visitor Center,** at Lafayette

Blvd. and Sunken Road; the **Fredericksburg National Cemetery,** where lie sixteen thousand Federal soldiers, nearly thirteen thousand of them unknown; **Chatham Manor,** a mansion used as Union headquarters during two of the battles, and later as a field hospital where Clara Barton and Walt Whitman nursed the wounded; and the **Stonewall Jackson Shrine** (twelve miles south on I-95 to Thornburg exit, then five miles east on VA 606 to Guinea), the plantation office where on May 10, 1863, Jackson died. All these sites are open daily, 9:00–5:00, and 8:30–6:30 during the summer. Admission is $3 for adults, free for children under seventeen. For information phone 540-371-0802.

SURPRISE THE BLUECOATS WITH JACKSON

Lee, badly outnumbered at Chancellorsville, gambled and won, sending Jackson's corps on a risky twelve-mile forced march around Hooker's Union army. Jackson took the Union by surprise and carried the day. You can follow in Jackson's footsteps along a gravel road for the first eight miles. The final miles are along a modern highway. Depending on your physical condition, the hike should take from three to four hours. (Be sure to have someone pick you up when you reach the highway, or it will be a long hike indeed.) Get directions and additional information at the **Chancellorsville Visitor Center,** 120 Chatham Lane, Fredericksburg, VA, open daily, 9:00–5:00. For information phone 540-786-2880.

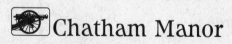

Chatham Manor

Fredericksburg, Virginia

While the owner of this magnificent mansion was away serving as a Confederate staff officer, the Federal army used it at various times as an artillery position; a communications center; the headquarters of several generals, including

Irwin McDowell, Ambrose Burnside, Edwin Sumner, and John
Gibbon; and a field hospital with the help of Clara Barton, Walt
Whitman, and Dr. Mary Walker, the only woman to be awarded
the Medal of Honor. Lincoln dined with General McDowell at
Chatham while visiting Fredericksburg during the Peninsular
Campaign. Yankee soldiers treated the place roughly, using the
original paneling as firewood, drawing graffiti on exposed
plaster, and riding horses through the first floor.

Chatham was built in 1767–1768 by William Fitzhugh, a
staunch supporter of the American cause in the Revolution,
and George Washington was a frequent guest. Some historians
believe that it was here that Robert E. Lee met his bride to be,
Mary Custis, the daughter of George Washington Parke Custis,
the grandson of Martha Washington and the adopted son of
George Washington.

Chatham Manor, now part of the Fredericksburg and
Spotsylvania National Military Park, is open daily, 9:00–5:00,
except Christmas and New Year's Day. Admission is $3 for
adults, free for children under seventeen. Five of the ten
rooms are open to the public. To reach the property from
Fredericksburg take Rte. 3 across the Chatham Bridge, turn
left at the first light, then take the next left to Chatham. For
information phone 540-371-0802.

The Richard Johnston Inn

Fredericksburg, Virginia

In 1861 this was a quiet town of five thousand inhabitants, on
a railroad and protected by the Rappahannock and Rapi-
dan Rivers. Its strategic location, midway between Washington
and Richmond, made it a barrier to a Union invasion of the
Confederacy. Engulfed by the war, the town would change
hands seven times. Four great battles were fought in and

around Fredericksburg. The battles, in which casualties totaled more than 100,000, were distinguished by the military genius of Robert E. Lee.

In the heart of Fredericksburg, across from the **Visitor Center,** is the Richard Johnston Inn, the namesake of the mayor of Fredericksburg who lived here in the early 1800s. It is a charming 1787 brick row house with a third-floor dormer and a patio that adjoins the parking lot in the rear. One look inside and you know owner Susan Williams has restored and furnished her inn with loving care. Chippendale and Empire-style antiques grace the common room downstairs. The guest rooms include two suites with living rooms, wet bars, and private entrances opening onto the patio. Breakfast is served in the dining room with china, crystal, and silver.

Address: 711 Caroline St., Fredericksburg, VA 22401; tel: 540-899-7606.
Accommodations: Six double rooms and two suites, all with private baths.
Amenities: Air-conditioning, off-street parking, cable TV in three guest rooms. Two friendly dogs in residence.
Rates: $$–$$$, including continental breakfast. American Express, Visa, MasterCard, and personal checks.
Restrictions: No pets, no smoking.

The Kenmore Inn
Fredericksburg, Virginia

This building in the historic district, which dates from the late 1700s, took a pounding during the Battle of Fredericksburg, and evidence of the heavy Union shelling is still evident in the roof supports. It was a family dwelling then and remained one until the early 1930s, when it was expanded and made into a small hotel.

Today, it is a gracious and luxurious inn, perfectly located for guests to explore the Civil War battlefields and historic buildings in Fredericksburg and the surrounding area. The guest rooms are warm and comfortable, with working fireplaces, decanters of sherry, and tea and cookies in the afternoon. The inn has an excellent restaurant and a pub with live music on the weekends.

Innkeeper Edward Bannon does a fine job of keeping everything as it should be. The **Fredericksburg Visitor Center** is a short walk away, and the streets abound with antique shops. No one who is interested in the Civil War should miss Fredericksburg; no one who enjoys gracious living should miss the Kenmore Inn.

Address: 1200 Princess Anne St., Fredericksburg, VA 22401; tel: 540-371-7622; fax: 540-371-5480.
Accommodations: Twelve guest rooms, all with private baths.
Amenities: Fireplaces and canopy beds in some rooms, sherry, tea, and cookies in the afternoon, TV in lounge, dining room, and pub.
Rates: $$–$$$. The Modified American Plan, which includes breakfast and dinner in the rate, is available with two-day stay. All major credit cards and personal checks.
Restrictions: No pets, restricted smoking.

La Vista Plantation

Fredericksburg, Virginia

About six miles from this 1838 plantation house in the countryside south of Fredericksburg is the Stonewall Jackson Shrine, the building where he died after being accidentally wounded by his own men at the Battle of Chancellorsville.

La Vista has also seen a lot of history. After the Battle of Spotsylvania, the Fourth Corps of the Union army came through the nearby fields like a swarm of angry bees. And Stonewall's ghost may be in residence here, perhaps because the bed in which he died was stored here for many years.

The present owners of La Vista, Michele and Edward Schiesser, who is the chief of exhibits and design at the Hirshhorn Museum in Washington, report that a sound near the front door is heard "virtually every other day." On other occasions they have heard someone, or something, stomping upstairs. Guests tell of whispers when no one else was in the room, and of a soldier standing in the front yard. However, all this merely adds a dash of mystery to a visit to this inn.

The inn has high ceilings, heart-of-pine floors, acorn moldings, and a handsome two-story portico. On the ten-acre grounds is a pond stocked with bass. The bedroom on the main floor has a king-size mahogany four-poster. The bedroom in the English basement has a queen-size cherry pencil post bed, a double bed, and a sitting room with a queen sleep sofa, and easily accommodates a small family. Both bedrooms have working fireplaces.

Address: 4420 Guinea Station Rd., Fredericksburg, VA 22408; tel: 540-898-8444 or 800-529-2823; fax: 540-898-9414; E-mail: LAVISTABB@aol.com.

Accommodations: One bedroom and one apartment, both with private baths.

Amenities: Air-conditioning, off-street parking; phone, TV, and refrigerator in rooms, complimentary ice and sodas, golf and tennis nearby.

Rates: $$. Visa, MasterCard, and personal checks.

Restrictions: No pets, no smoking.

The Stonewall Jackson Shrine

Guinea Station, Virginia

As darkness fell on the Battle of Chancellorsville, Stonewall Jackson was mortally wounded by shots mistakenly fired by his own troops. He was taken to a field hospital near Wilderness Tavern, where his left arm was amputated. Lee sent word to him, "You have lost your left arm, I have lost my right."

On May 4, Jackson endured a twenty-seven-mile ambulance ride to Fairfield Plantation at Guinea Station and was placed in a small office building by the railroad. The plan was to take Jackson by train to Richmond after he regained sufficient strength. But he contracted pneumonia, his condition worsened, and he died on May 10, 1863, after murmuring,

"Let us pass over the river, and rest under the shade of the trees."

The Stonewall Jackson Shrine is twelve miles south of Fredericksburg on I-95 to the Thornburg exit, then five miles east on VA 606. It is part of and administered by the Fredericksburg and Spotsylvania National Military Park. The small bedroom on the second floor of the building is as it was the day Jackson passed away. The shrine is open daily, 9:00–5:00, from mid-June to Labor Day; Friday–Monday, March to mid-June and Labor Day through October; weekends the rest of the year. Admission is $3 for adults, free for children under seventeen. For information phone 540-371-0802.

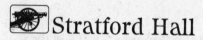 # Stratford Hall

Stratford, Virginia

This plantation, one of the grandest in Virginia, was the ancestral home of the Lees. Thomas Lee built the house in the 1730s, and here Robert E. Lee was born on January 19, 1807. Four years later his father's disastrous speculation in land left him virtually penniless, forcing him to move the family to Alexandria. All his adult life Robert E. Lee dreamed of owning Stratford Hall, but it was not to be. The house is an H-shaped fortress-like mansion with imposing chimney clusters. The southeast bedroom, called the Mother's Room, is where many of the Lee children, including Robert, were born. Lee's cradle is by the window. The house is furnished throughout with period antiques and family portraits. The plantation, originally encompassing sixteen thousand acres, now consists of sixteen hundred. The many original outbuildings include the kitchen, smokehouse, coach house, grist mill, slave quarters, and stables. The restored boxwood gardens are handsome.

Stratford Hall is a forty-five-minute drive east of Fredericksburg. Take Rte. 218 and VA 3 to Montross, then drive six miles north on Rte. 3, then east on Rte. 214. It is open daily, 9:00–4:30, except Thanksgiving, Christmas, and New Year's Day. The **Visitor Center** has a museum and a theater with an audiovisual presentation. Costumed docents conduct tours. A plantation lunch is served, 11:00–3:00. Admission is $7 for adults, $6 for seniors, and $3 for children. For information phone 804-493-8038.

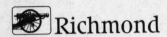

Richmond

Virginia

Richmond was the symbol of the Confederacy. It was the seat of its government, its largest manufacturing center, and the primary supply depot for troops operating on the Confederacy's northern frontier.

Early in the war, the North decided that if Richmond could be captured, the South would sue for peace. Seven major campaigns were launched against Richmond, two of which brought Union armies within sight of the city. The first was George B. McClellan's Peninsular Campaign of 1862, which was thwarted by Robert E. Lee. During the series of battles called the Seven Days, Lee sent the Union army reeling back toward Washington. In 1864, though, Ulysses S. Grant's crushing overland campaign finally captured Richmond, and the Confederacy came tumbling down.

There is clearly much of Civil War interest to see and do in Richmond. One of the most important sites is the **Richmond National Battlefield Park,** which consists of ten units comprising 770 acres. Start at the **Chimborazo Visitor Center,** 3215 E. Broad St. It occupies the site of the Confederacy's largest hospital, Chimborazo. Considered a medical marvel, it accommodated the flood of wounded arriving daily in the city, a total of nearly 76,000 during the war.

At the **Visitor Center,** museum, exhibits, and an audio-visual program depict the complexity of the defense of Richmond. The center also is the first stop on a fifty-six-mile, self-guided auto tour of the park. It takes a full day and includes sites associated with both the 1862 and 1864 campaigns. A map available at the center shows visitors how to select their own route, visiting some or all of the sites. Time permitting, the sites of the 1862 campaign should be visited on one day, the 1864 sites on another. The **Visitor Center** is open daily, 9:00–5:00. For information phone 804-226-1981.

The 1862 campaign sites include **Chickahominy Bluff,** where Lee watched the beginning of the Seven Days' Battles; **Beaver Dam Creek,** part of the three-mile Union front that the Confederates unsuccessfully assaulted; **Watt House,** on the **Gaines's Mill Battlefield,** which was the headquarters of General Fitz-John Porter during a crucial point in the fighting; **Malvern Hill,** where the last battle of the Seven Days was fought; and **Drewry's Bluff,** where Confederate cannon guarded the James River approach to Richmond.

The 1864 campaign sites on the tour include **Cold Harbor,** where Grant suffered terrible losses while attacking Lee's well-entrenched position, and **Fort Harrison,** a key position captured by Grant.

A Richmond treasure is the **White House of the Confederacy,** the home of President Davis and his family until Richmond fell in April 1865. The handsome house contains many original furnishings and personal items. Ten rooms have been restored to their wartime appearance, and the first floor contains a central parlor where the Davises entertained. Davis's offices and the family bedrooms are on the second floor.

The adjacent **Museum of the Confederacy** contains the nation's largest collection of Confederate weapons, uniforms, battle flags, letters, diaries, photographs, equipment, and other artifacts. Among the displays are Lee's field equipment, a model of the ironclad *Virginia,* made by a crewman, the sword Lee wore at the surrender, and Jeb Stuart's plumed hat.

Both attractions are open Monday–Saturday, 10:00–5:00, and Sunday, 12:00–5:00. A combined ticket is $8 for adults, $7 for seniors, and $5 for ages six through college. For information phone 804-649-1861.

Many important events of the war occurred in the **State Capitol,** on Capitol Square one block south of Broad St. For example, Virginia ratified the Articles of Secession, Lee assumed command of all Virginia forces, and the Confederate Congress met in the building. Open daily, 9:00–5:00, except Thanksgiving, Christmas, and New Year's Day; December through March, open Sunday, 1:00–5:00. Thirty-minute tours are available, the last one beginning at 4:00. Admission is free. For information phone 804-698-1788.

Saint Paul's Episcopal Church, southwest corner of Grace and Ninth, was known as the "Church of the Confederacy." President Davis received confirmation in the Episcopal faith here early into the war, and he was attending a service on April 2, 1865, when he received a message from Lee that the Petersburg defenses had been broken and Richmond had to be evacuated. Open daily, 10:00–4:00. For information phone 804-643-3589.

Battle Abbey, 428 North Blvd., was built in 1913 as a Confederate memorial. It is now the home of the Virginia Historical Society and their **Museum of Virginia**. Among other exhibits, the museum boasts the Maryland-Steuart Collection of Confederate-made weapons, considered to be the world's finest. There is a library onsite and educational programs are offered daily. A mammoth mural series by Charles Hoffbauer depicts *The Four Seasons of the Confederacy*. Open daily, 10:00–5:00, except Sunday, 1:00–5:00. Admission is $4 for adults, $3 for seniors, and $2 for children and students. For information phone 804-358-4901.

Hollywood Cemetery, 412 S. Cherry St. at Albermarle. The notables buried here include James Monroe, John Tyler, Jefferson Davis, and J. E. B. Stuart. Some fifteen thousand

Confederate soldiers are also interred in the 115-acre cemetery, which was opened in 1853. The cemetery office at the
gate offers an audiovisual program and a map showing the
location of the prominent graves. Open daily. For information
phone 804-648-8501.

Linden Row Inn

Richmond, Virginia

The Greek Revival town houses that make up what is known
as Linden Row have been a Richmond landmark since
1847. They shared a garden that was the childhood play-
ground of Edgar Allan Poe and the inspiration for the
"enchanted garden" in his poems. During the war, the two
westernmost houses were occupied by the Southern Female
Institute, and President Jefferson Davis riding by on horseback
was a familiar morning sight.

Linden Row is rated an AAA Four Diamond Inn, and is
listed on the National Register. Furnished in the Victorian
style, the inn's original features include fireplaces with marble
mantels and crystal chandeliers. Snacks and refreshments are
served on the patio, and the dining room features Southern
cuisine. Guests enjoy a complimentary wine and cheese reception in the parlor. The inn is within walking distance of the
Capitol, the Museum and White House of the Confederacy,
and the Valentine Museum.

Address: 100 E. Franklin St., Richmond, VA 23219;
  tel: 804-783-7000; fax: 804-648-7504.
Accommodations: Seventy guest rooms (including seven
  parlor suites), all with private baths.
Amenities: Climate-controlled rooms, cable TV and clock-
  radio in rooms, afternoon refreshments, use of nearby fitness
  center, valet parking, free transportation to downtown.

Rates: $$ in garden court, $$$ in main house, including continental breakfast. All major credit cards and personal checks.
Restrictions: No pets, restricted smoking.

Emmanuel Hutzler House

Richmond, Virginia

Memories of the war were stirred in the capital city on May 7, 1890, when J. A. C. Mercie's statue of Robert E. Lee, hat in hand and astride his horse Traveller, was loaded on four gaily covered wagons and hauled by men, women, and children to its present location. It was dedicated three weeks later before a crowd of 100,000, unveiled by Joseph E. Johnston, assisted by Wade Hampton and Fitzhugh Lee. The only inscription on the statue is LEE. The statue was erected on the newly laid out Monument Avenue, a broad mall that would become the city's boulevard of honor, lined by handsome mansions.

One mansion, of Italian Renaissance design and a few steps away from the Lee statue, now houses this comfortable inn. Mahogany paneling is used extensively in its eight-thousand-square-foot interior, and innkeepers Lyn Benson and John Richardson have furnished it with period pieces. They have retained the best of the past, while adding such modern-day amenities as air-conditioning and new bathrooms.

Address: 2036 Monument Ave., Richmond VA 23220; tel: 804-353-6900 or 804-355-4885; fax: 804-355-5053.
Accommodations: Four double rooms, all with private baths, two with Jacuzzis.
Amenities: Air-conditioning, off-street parking, phone and TV in rooms.
Rates: $$–$$$. All major credit cards and personal checks.
Restrictions: No children under twelve, no pets (pet boarding nearby), no smoking.

The William Catlin House

Richmond, Virginia

This house in the historic Church Hill District was built in 1845 for William Catlin by one of the finest masons in the country. A block away is St. John's Church, where Patrick Henry demanded "liberty or death." The inn also is convenient to the Virginia State Capitol, where Lee was sworn in as commander of Virginia's armed forces in the Civil War, and Shockoe Slip with its restaurants and shops.

Now the house is an inn, richly appointed with antiques and family heirlooms and hosted by Robert and Josephine Martin, who live in the house to make sure everything runs smoothly. Guests are pampered with bedroom fireplaces, goose-down pillows, and, at night, a chocolate mint and a glass of sherry. Coffee or tea is waiting in the morning, and the full breakfast is a testament to Southern hospitality. For an informal dinner try the restaurant at Mr. Patrick Henry's Inn next door (804-644-1322).

Address: 2304 E. Broad St., Richmond, VA 23223; tel: 804-780-3746.

Accommodations: Five bedrooms, three with private baths and two with shared bath.

Amenities: Air-conditioning, fireplaces in rooms.

Rates: $$, including full breakfast. Visa, MasterCard, Discover, and personal checks.

Restrictions: No pets, no smoking.

Berkeley Plantation

Charles City County, Virginia

This plantation on the north bank of the James River was the home of the Harrisons, the prominent Virginia family that included a signer of the Declaration of Independence and two presidents, William Henry Harrison and Benjamin Harrison. The land was part of a royal grant in 1619; the house was built in 1726. In 1862, General McClellan established his Peninsular Campaign headquarters here. Lincoln came to Berkeley twice to consult with McClellan and review the 140,000 troops that were camped nearby. While here, General Daniel Butterfield composed the bugle call "Taps." After Lee drove McClellan from the gates of Richmond in the Seven Days' Battles, McClellan's army retreated here to board ships to return to Washington. In 1907, Berkeley was purchased by John Jamieson, who had camped at the plantation when he was a drummer boy with the Union forces. The house has been restored and furnished with period pieces.

Berkeley Plantation, off Rte. 5, about a thirty-minute drive from Richmond, is open daily, 8:00–5:00, except Christmas. An audiovisual presentation is a prelude to a tour of the house and grounds. Admission is $8.50 for adults, $7.65 for seniors, $6.50 for children thirteen to sixteen, and $4 for children six to twelve. The Coach House Restaurant serves lunch daily and dinner by reservation only. For information phone 804-829-6018.

Shirley Plantation

Charles City County, Virginia

This handsome, three-story brick house on the James River
was the ancestral home of Robert E. Lee's mother, Anne
Carter Lee. After his father suffered financial reverses, the boy
lived here for a while and attended the plantation school with
his cousins. During the Civil War, wounded Federal troops were
brought to the lawn around the house after the nearby Battle of
Malvern Hill. One Carter resident wrote that "they lay all about
on this lawn and all up and down the river bank. Nurses went
about with buckets of water and ladles for them to drink and
bathe their faces . . . Mama had to tear up sheets and pillow cases
to bind their wounds, and we made them soup and bread every
day until they died or were carried away." General McClellan
sent a letter, "with the highest respect," thanking the Carters for
their aid to men "whom you probably regard as bitter foes."

Shirley Plantation is off Rte. 5, in Charles City County, a
forty-minute drive from downtown Richmond. It is open daily,
9:00–5:00, except Thanksgiving, Christmas, and New Year's
Day. Docents lead tours of the house and grounds. Admission
is $8.50 for adults, $7.50 for seniors, AAA members, and military, $5.50 for youths thirteen to twenty-one, and $4.50 for
children six to twelve. For information phone 804-829-5121.

Edgewood Plantation

Charles City, Virginia

This Gothic house was built in 1849 on land that once
belonged to the nearby Berkeley Plantation, and Confederate officers used the third floor to spy on McClellan's troops
when they were camped at Berkeley in 1862. On June 15 of

that year, Jeb Stuart stopped by for coffee on his way to Richmond to apprise Lee of the disposition and strength of Federal troops.

The house was built for Spencer Rowland, and one of his daughters scratched her nickname "Lizzie" on the window in one of the bedrooms, where she later died of a broken heart when her lover was killed in the war. Two of the guest rooms are in the slave quarters behind the house; they overlook English gardens and the millrace canal dug by slaves in the 1700s. Over the years the house has been a church, post office, telephone exchange, nursing home, and a restaurant. Now the National Landmark has been modernized, restored to its original glory, and furnished with antiques and period reproductions. Edgewood is an ideal place to stay while exploring the other grand plantations along the James.

Address: 4800 John Tyler Memorial Highway, Charles City, VA 23023; tel: 804-829-2962 or 800-296-3343.
Accommodations: Eight guest rooms, seven with private baths.
Amenities: Air-conditioning, parking area, TV in rooms, billiard room, gift shop, swimming pool.
Rates: $$$. All major credit cards and personal checks.
Restrictions: No children, no pets, restricted smoking.

North Bend Plantation

Charles City, Virginia

General Philip Sheridan made his headquarters at this plantation in 1864 and his troops dug defensive trenches across its fields to the James River. Their breastworks can still be seen on the eastern edge of the property. The main house contains many mementos of Civil War days. The plantation desk has the original labels on its pigeonholes. Sheridan's map of the area now hangs in the billiard room.

The present owner of North Bend, George Copland, is the great-grandson of the wartime owner, Edmund Ruffin, who is credited with firing the first shot of the war at Fort Sumter, in April 1861. Copland and his wife have restored the home and grounds to their original beauty. Federal-style mantels and stair carvings survive from the oldest portion of the house, which was built in 1819 for the sister of William Harrison, the ninth president. Also surviving are all the Greek revival features from the 1853 remodeling and many family heirlooms and memorabilia. Of particular interest is a collection of rare books, including volumes of *Harpers Pictorial History of the Civil War*, copyright 1869.

Address: 12200 Weyanoke Rd., Charles City, VA 23030; tel: 804-829-5176 or 800-841-1479; fax: 804-829-6828.
Accommodations: Four guest rooms, all with private baths.
Amenities: Air-conditioning, ceiling fans; billiard room, library, croquet, horseshoes, and a swimming pool are on the premises.
Rates: $$$. Visa, MasterCard, and personal checks.
Restrictions: No children under six, no pets, restricted smoking.

Petersburg Battlefield

Petersburg, Virginia

After an unsuccessful attempt at Cold Harbor to take Richmond by a frontal attack, Grant withdrew and attacked Petersburg. After four days of hard fighting failed to break the Confederate lines, he gave up and laid siege to the city.

Lee couldn't afford to abandon Petersburg; it was the rail center that furnished his troops with supplies. If it fell, Richmond would surely fall, too. The siege lasted ten months, from June 15, 1864, to April 2, 1865, with the two armies in almost

constant contact. When Petersburg finally fell, Lee's surrender at Appomattox was only a week away.

The **Petersburg National Battlefield,** on Rte. 36, two miles east of the city off I-95, preserves Union and Confederate fortifications, trenches, and gun pits. A second unit of the park, **Five Forks Unit,** is located twenty-three miles to the west. It was at Five Forks that Sheridan's troopers broke through Confederate defenses, which led to the fall of Petersburg and Lee's retreat. The park is open daily, 8:00–5:50 in the summer, 8:00–5:00 the rest of the year, and is closed for Presidents' Day, Martin Luther King Day, Thanksgiving, Christmas, and New Year's Day.

Maps for the self-guided auto tour are available at the **Visitor Center**. Living history programs are presented daily during the summer. Admission is $4 for adults, free for children sixteen and under. For information phone 804-732-3531.

Other sites of interest in the Petersburg area include the **Blandford Church and Cemetery,** which has thirteen Louis Comfort Tiffany stained-glass windows celebrating the thirteen states of the Confederacy; the windows were donated by the individual states in memory of the thirty thousand Confederate soldiers buried in the cemetery.

The **City Point Unit** of the National Battlefield is where, between June 1864 and April 1865, the sleepy village of City Point was transformed into a bustling supply center for the 100,000 Federal troops on the siege lines. On the grounds of the Appomattox Plantation in City Point is the cabin Grant used as his headquarters during the siege.

FOLLOW LEE'S RETREAT FROM PETERSBURG TO APPOMATTOX

With the fall of Petersburg, Lee retreated across the area called Southside Virginia, Grant in hot pursuit. Now you can follow Lee's route, visiting the sites that played a role in the drama. The 140-mile driving tour takes at least a day. For a map of the route phone 1-800-6-RETREAT. An interpretive radio message at each stop is broadcast on 1610 AM.

Start at the **Petersburg Visitor Center** in the Old Towne Petersburg historic district, where you can pick up a map of the Retreat as well as books and an audiotape. Beside the Visitor-Center is:

1. South Railroad Station (April 2). Lee's troops evacuated Petersburg in and around the station after the last supply line was cut. Follow the red, white, and blue trailblazing signs to:

2. Pamplin Park Civil War Site (April 2). At dawn the Federal troops attacked and finally broke Lee's defensive line. Follow the signs to:

3. Sutherland Station (April 2). Grant's forces severed the South Side Railroad here, Lee's last supply line into Petersburg. Now take Rte. 708 to:

4. Namozine Church (April 3). As Lee's soldiers marched toward Amelia Court House, a rearguard cavalry skirmish took place around this church. Continue on Rte. 708, then right on Rte. 153, and turn left on Rte. 38 and drive about five miles to:

5. Amelia Court House (April 4–5). Confederate troops from Petersburg and Richmond assembled here, hoping to continue on to North Carolina and link up with Johnston's army. About six miles southwest on Rte. 360 is:

6. Jetersville (April 5). Lee ran into Union forces here and changed his route to go toward Farmville. Continue on Rte. 642 for about six miles to:

7. Amelia Springs (April 6). Here the Federals came in contact with the rebel rearguard as Lee completed a night march to avoid Grant's forces at Jetersville. Continue for about three miles, turning left on Rte. 617, to:

8. Deatonville (April 6). A brief rearguard action was fought here on the way to Farmville. About two miles along the road is:

9. Holt's Corner (April 6). At this road junction, part of Lee's army turned while the main force continued ahead to the crossing of Little Sayler's Creek. Continue on Rte. 617 to:

10. Hillsman House (April 6). Near this house, which was used as a field hospital, was fought the Battle of Sayler's Creek, the last major battle of the Army of the Potomac and the Army of Northern Virginia. Federal troops captured more than seven thousand prisoners, a fifth of Lee's army. Stunned, Lee said: "My God! Has the army dissolved?" About a mile farther is:

11. Marshall's Crossroads (April 6). While the battle raged at Sayler's Creek, Union cavalry fought Confederate infantry here. Double back to Rte. 618 at Holt's Corner, turn left, go to Rte. 619, turn left, and drive on to:

12. Lockett House (April 6). Numerous bullet holes attest to the fighting that took place near the creek close to the house. The house was later used as a field hospital. Proceed on Rte. 619 to:

13. Double Bridges (April 6). The Confederate wagon train and column that turned off at Holt's Corner became bogged down in crossing Sayler's Creek here and were attacked by Federal forces. Five miles south on Rte. 619 after it crosses Rte. 307 is:

14. Rice's Depot (April 6). Lee's men dug in here to protect the road and skirmished with Federal troops coming from the direction of Burkeville Junction. Proceed to Rte. 460 to:

15. Cavalry Battle at High Bridge (April 6). Some nine hundred Federal troopers, on a mission to burn this South Side Railroad trestle over the Appomattox River, were intercepted and most of them captured. Four miles down the road is:

16. Farmville (April 7). Both armies marched through this tobacco town. Lee, hoping to issue rations to his troops here, was unsuccessful and crossed to the north side of the Appomattox River. Three miles north on Rte. 45 is:

17. Cumberland Church (April 7). Federal forces that had crossed the river at High Bridge attacked Lee's forces around this church and forced him to delay his march until nightfall. Turn right on Rte. 657 and drive two miles to:

18. High Bridge (April 7). Confederate forces had burned four spans of this bridge, but failed to destroy the lower wagon bridge. This enabled the Federals to continue the pursuit of Lee's army north of the Appomattox. Circle back to Rte. 636 and proceed to the crossing of Rte. 15.

19. Clifton (April 8). Generals Grant and Meade used this location for their headquarters during the night. Grant stayed in the house and it was here he received Lee's second letter suggesting a peace meeting. He left the next morning and rode on to Appomattox Court House. Continue on Rte. 636 to:

20. New Store (April 8). At this point, General Lee's army would change its line of march. They would continue to be pursued by two Union army corps. Take Rte. 636 to Rte. 24, turn left, and go to:

21. Lee's Rearguard (April 8). Here General Longstreet built breastworks to protect the rear of Lee's army, most of which was four miles south at Appomattox Court House. Continue on Rte. 24, past the National Historic Park to the town of Appomattox.

22. Battle of Appomattox Station (April 8). In the evening, Union cavalry captured four trains of supplies at the station intended for Lee's army. Later, after a brief engagement, they also captured portions of the Confederate wagon train and twenty-five cannon.

23–26. As an alternate route in driving from Petersburg to Appomattox, following Rte. 460, are stops 23–26: Burkeville (April 5–May 1865); Crewe (April 5–6, 1865); Nottoway Court House (April 5, 1865); and Battle of Nottoway (June 23, 1864).

The Owl and the Pussycat

Petersburg, Virginia

A local merchant, John Gill, built this brick Queen Anne-style mansion in 1895, and his descendants occupied it until the 1940s. Now it is an attractive inn, two blocks from the Siege Museum, fifteen minutes from the Petersburg Battlefield, and a half-hour or so drive from the plantations of the lower James River.

The present owners, John and Juliette Swenson, had owned a bed-and-breakfast in Port Townsend, Washington, before coming here. The inn was named after Edward Lear's famous children's poem, and the guest rooms reflect the theme: the Owl Room includes the turret of the house, which overlooks the front garden; the Pussycat Room has a collection of teapots; and the Sonnet Room has a collection of books of poetry. Mrs. Swenson, who grew up in Bath, England, often serves Sally Lunn bread with breakfast.

Address: 405 High St., Petersburg, VA 23803;
  tel: 804-733-0505; fax: 804-862-0694;
  E-mail: owlcat@ctg.net.
Accommodations: Six guest rooms, two share a bath.
Amenities: Air-conditioning, off-street parking, TV in common
  room, sun room, badminton, croquet.
Rates: $$, including full breakfast on weekends, continental
  on weekdays. All major credit cards and personal checks.
Restrictions: $20 cleaning deposit required for pets, no
  smoking.

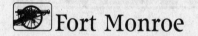

Fort Monroe

Fort Monroe, Virginia

This is the largest stone fort ever built in the United States. Construction began in 1819, and four years later the fort received its first army garrison. In 1831, a young army engineer named Robert E. Lee arrived to help supervise the construction of the fort's moat.

When war came, the Confederacy did not attempt to seize Fort Monroe. As a result, Virginia had no fort throughout the war, which denied the state access to the sea.

Lincoln visited here to observe the Union attack on Norfolk, and later McClellan used the fort as the springboard for his Peninsular Campaign.

Jefferson Davis, captured after the war, was imprisoned here. First kept in a casement, a chamber in the wall of the

fort, he was moved to a room in the fort's officers' quarters, and released two years later. His cell, now a museum, has been restored to its appearance when Davis was imprisoned.

The **Casement Museum/Fort Monroe,** PO Box 51341, Fort Monroe, VA, is open daily, 10:30–4:30. Guided tours with two weeks' notice for groups of ten or more. To reach the fort from I-64, take Exit 268 and follow the signs to Fort Monroe. For information phone 757-727-3391.

Willow Grove Inn

Orange, Virginia

Confederate General A. P. Hill once made his headquarters in this classic plantation house, and the trenches and breastworks his men built are still visible on the spacious grounds. Willow Grove had seen war before. During the Revolution, generals Wayne and Muhlenberg camped here, and later Dolley Madison was a neighbor. The house is in the National Register and is a Virginia Historic Landmark.

The inn stands on a hill overlooking the meadows of the Piedmont region, near where three of the first five presidents lived: Jefferson, Madison, and Monroe. Seven guest rooms are named for Virginia-born presidents and furnished with period pieces.

Despite its impressive historical credentials, Willow Grove is a relaxed, friendly place to stay. What once was the root cellar is now a bar and the scene of weekend sing-alongs. On cold winter nights, fires burn in the fireplaces of the second-floor bedrooms. The meals here are exceptional. Dinner may include smoked Rappahannock trout, shank of venison, saddle of rabbit, local greens, and goat cheese. Particularly popular is the three-course brunch on Sunday.

Willow Grove is expensive, but few historic inns in the country measure up to it.

Address: 14079 Plantation Way, Orange, VA 22960; tel: 540-672-5982 or 800-949-1778; fax: 540-672-3674.

Accommodations: Eight double rooms and two suites, all with private baths.

Amenities: Air-conditioning, off-street parking, restaurant, pre-breakfast tray delivered to room. Civil War Camp reenactment during summer.

Rates: $$$, including full breakfast and dinner. All major credit cards and personal checks.

Restrictions: Notice required if bringing children. Pets allowed in cottages but not in main house. Restricted smoking.

Inn at Narrow Passage

Woodstock, Virginia

In March 1862, this inn served as Stonewall Jackson's headquarters during his Shenandoah Valley Campaign. It was here that Jackson ordered Jedediah Hotchkiss to "make me a map of the valley." (The extraordinary Hotchkiss maps are displayed in the Handley Library in Winchester.)

The inn wasn't new then; it has been welcoming travelers for more than 250 years. The oldest part of the inn was built around 1740, and its sturdy log walls were protection from Indian attacks at the Great Wagon Road's "narrow passage," where the roadbed was only wide enough for one wagon to pass through. A large addition was made to the inn around the time of the Revolutionary War.

Innkeepers Ellen and Ed Markel Jr. welcome guests with lemonade served on the porch. Rooms in the older part have pine floors and stenciling. Rooms in the later additions also are decorated in the colonial style, but open to porches, with views of the Shenandoah River and the Massanutten Mountains. Most rooms have fireplaces. A hearty breakfast is served by the fireplace in the dining room.

Address: PO Box 608, Woodstock, VA 22664; tel. 540-459-8000; fax: 540-459-8001.
Accommodations: Thirteen rooms, all with private baths.
Amenities: Air-conditioning, parking onsite, room phones, fishing and hiking, conference facilities.
Rates: $$–$$$. Visa, MasterCard, and personal checks.
Restrictions: No pets, restricted smoking.

Ashton Country House

Staunton, Virginia

Although Civil War artifacts have been unearthed near this inn, the town's main link to the war was musical. It was the home of the Fifth Virginia Regimental Band, which Stonewall Jackson appropriated and rechristened the Stonewall Brigade Band. At Appomattox, Grant allowed the musicians to take home their instruments, and they serenaded him when he passed through town after the war.

This inn, an 1860 Victorian house, is a good place to relax, and Staunton (pronounced Stanton by the natives) is near a number of Civil War-related sites in the lower Shenandoah Valley, including the New Market Battlefield, the Lee Chapel, and Stonewall Jackson's home in Lexington. The spacious house, furnished in the Empire style, has a forty-foot-long hall, high ceilings, and heart-of-pine floors. It is on twenty-five acres with goats and cows for neighbors. A secluded porch beckons those who just want to relax with a book. Hosts Vince and Dorie DiStefano greet guests with tea and home-baked goodies, and sherry and candy are placed in the guest rooms.

Address: 1205 Middlebrook Ave., Staunton, VA 24401; tel: 540-885-7819 or 800-296-7819.

Accommodations: Four double rooms, one suite, all with private baths.

Amenities: Central air-conditioning, off-street parking; TV, VCR, and fireplace in suite, fireplaces in three of the other rooms.

Rates: $$. Visa, MasterCard, and personal checks.

Restrictions: Children accepted with notice, no pets, no smoking.

Stonewall Jackson House

Lexington, Virginia

Stonewall Jackson lived in Lexington and taught at the Virginia Military Institute during the 1850s. He and his second wife, Mary Anna Morrison, moved into this house in 1859, the only house he ever owned. After the war, the house was used as a hospital for a number of years before being opened to visitors. Now a National Historic Landmark, the house and garden have been restored to their appearance of 1859–61. A number of Jackson's personal effects are on display in the house.

Jackson and hundreds of his compatriots are buried in the **Stonewall Jackson Memorial Cemetery,** on South Main St. The great general's grave is marked by a full-length statue by Edward V. Valentine.

The **Stonewall Jackson House,** 8 E. Washington St., Lexington, VA 24450, is open Monday–Saturday, 9:00–5:00, to 6:00 in July and August, Sunday 1:00–5:00. Admission is $5 for adults, $2.50 for children six to twelve, free for children under six. Interpretive audiovisual program. Guided tours. For information phone 540-463-2552.

Virginia Military Institute

Lexington, Virginia

Next door to Washington and Lee University is the Virginia Military Institute, founded in 1839, the first state military college in the country. The school contributed a host of officers and men to the Confederate cause, including Lee's most trusted lieutenant, Thomas "Stonewall" Jackson, who taught physics and artillery tactics here before the war. His statue now

stands at the center of the campus, overlooking the parade ground, with the four cannons he named Matthew, Mark, Luke, and John. On the east side of the parade ground is Sir Moses Ezekiel's seated statue of *Virginia Mourning Her Dead*, a monument to the ten VMI cadets who were killed in the 1864 Battle of New Market. Mementos of Jackson are on display in the campus museum, including the raincoat he was wearing when he was fatally shot at Chancellorsville. The bullet hole is clearly visible.

The **Virginia Military Institute** campus and museum are open daily except Thanksgiving and December 20–January 10. Admission is free. Dress parades are held Friday afternoons, September through May, weather permitting. For information phone 540-464-7000.

Llewellyn Lodge

Lexington, Virginia

Civil War buffs have a lot to see in Lexington—the Lee Chapel and the house Stonewall Jackson lived in when he taught at the Virginia Military Institute. And there are many antique shops to explore.

This handsome Colonial revival house has been a bed-and-breakfast since the early 1940s; in fact, it's the oldest such establishment in town. Guests receive a warm welcome from hosts John and Ellen Roberts. In the summer expect lemonade or iced tea on the porch; in the winter it's John's "killer" hot chocolate or hot spiced cider by the fire and, of course, cookies. Ellen's breakfasts are a local legend and John can lead you to the best trout streams and hiking trails in the area.

Address: 603 S. Main St., Lexington, VA 24450;
tel: 540-463-3235 or 800-882-1145; fax: 540-464-3122;
E-mail: LLL@rockbridge.net.
Accommodations: Six double rooms, all with private baths.
Amenities: Air-conditioning, off-street parking, public golf and tennis a mile away, fly-fishing nearby, concierge service.
Rates: $$. Senior discount, Monday–Thursday. All major credit cards and personal checks.
Restrictions: No children under ten, no pets, no smoking.

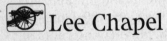 Lee Chapel

Washington and Lee University
Lexington, Virginia

Robert E. Lee was president of what now is Washington and Lee University. He assumed the position shortly after the war and served until his death five years later at the age of sixty-three. He was not simply a figurehead. He worked hard

to lift the academic standards and increase the enrollment of the little college. His unpretentious office in the basement of the Lee Chapel on the campus remains intact, chairs still drawn up around a small conference table. Down the hall from the office Lee's remains are entombed in a family crypt, and family mementos are displayed in a small museum. In the Chapel, upstairs, are hung the Pine portrait of Lee and the Peale portrait of the young George Washington, as well as the famous recumbent statue of Lee sculpted by Edward V. Valentine. Lee lies with one hand on his chest, his face tranquil but ravaged by the years of war. The remains of his beloved horse, Traveller, are buried outside the chapel. A few steps away from the chapel is the house where the Lees lived in those years.

The **Lee Chapel** is open Monday–Saturday, 9:00–4:00, Sunday, 2:00–5:00, except New Year's Day, Thanksgiving, and the following Friday. Admission is free. For information phone 540-463-8400.

Red Shutter Farmhouse

New Market, Virginia

On May 15, 1864, a desperate General John Breckinridge ordered 247 cadets from the Virginia Military Institute to join the battle against the forces of Federal general Franz Sigel. The boys entered the fray fearlessly, and their heroism inspired the victory of the Confederate troops.

Five miles south of the battlefield, next to the Endless Caverns, is this friendly bed-and-breakfast on twenty acres, owned and hosted by George and Juanita Miller. The main house was built in 1790 and enlarged in 1870, 1920, and 1930. Guests are offered a variety of large rooms, all furnished in the Virginia country style.

Address: Rte. 1, PO Box 376, New Market, VA 22844;
  tel: 540-740-4281; fax: 540-740-4661.
Accommodations: Five double rooms, three with private baths.
Amenities: Air-conditioning, off-street parking, afternoon tea,
  TV and game room, hiking, nearby golf, horseback riding,
  antique and craft shops.
Rates: $$. Visa, MasterCard, and personal checks.
Restrictions: No pets, restricted smoking.

New Market Battlefield

New Market, Virginia

On May 15, 1864, a large Federal force on its way to plunder the supply depot at Staunton was met by General John Breckinridge leading five thousand hastily assembled troops, including 247 cadets from the Virginia Military Institute. The outcome was in doubt until Breckinridge reluctantly ordered the cadets into battle. The boys charged the Federal line, making possible a Confederate victory.

The **Hall of Valor** here has exhibits tracing the events of the war, and audiovisual presentations on Jackson's 1862 campaign and the VMI heroes. The **New Market Battlefield Park and Hall of Valor** are open daily. From I-81 take Exit 264 (New Market), go west on Rte. 211, then right on Collins Dr. (Rte. 305). Admission is $6 for adults, $5 for seniors, and $2 for children six to fifteen. For information phone 540-740-3101.

The **New Market Battlefield Military Museum** is on Manor's Hill, where the fiercest fighting took place. Each side held a position on the hill until the Federals were forced to retreat north. The victory here was the last Confederate victory in the Shenandoah Valley. The museum has over three thousand artifacts ranging from the Revolutionary War to the Gulf War, with a focus on the Civil War. From I-81 take Exit 264 at New Market, turn west; turn right at next road (Collins Dr.). Travel a quarter of a mile. Museum entrance is on left at top of hill. A thirty-five-minute film on the war is shown hourly. Visitors can take a self-guided walking tour of the battlefield, following historical markers. Open March 15 through December 1, daily 9:00–5:00. Admission is $6 for adults, $5 for seniors, and $2 for children. For information phone 540-740-8065.

The **Museum of the American Cavalry,** 298 W. Old Crossroads, has an extensive collection of cavalry-related items: guns, sabers, and uniforms, with special emphasis on the Civil War. From I-81 take Exit 264 and turn west on Rte. 211, then make an immediate right onto Collins Dr. Museum is on the left. Open April through November, daily, 9:00–5:00. Admission is $4.50 for adults, $2.50 for children. For information phone 540-740-3959.

Chester

Scottsville, Virginia

Late in the war, during Sheridan's devastating Shenandoah Valley campaign, Major James Hill was wounded while commanding the local Confederate forces. While recuperating here at Chester, he was visited by General Sheridan and his aide, Colonel George Armstrong Custer. Believing Hill was a dying man, they decided not to arrest him. Hill fooled them, however, and lived to become a general and editor of the local newspaper after the war.

This beautiful house was built in 1847 by a retired landscape architect from Chester, England. Chester's eight acres contain a lily pond, stands of English boxwood, and upward of fifty different varieties of shrubs and flowers.

Innkeepers Craig and Jean Stratton have given Chester an elegant charm that befits an English inn. Convenient to Jefferson's Monticello, Monroe's Ash Lawn, Michie Tavern, and the other attractions in the Charlottesville area, Chester provides an intimate setting for comfort and relaxation.

Address: 243 James River Rd., Scottsville, VA 24590; tel: 804-286-3960.

Accommodations: Five double rooms, all with private baths and fireplaces.

Amenities: Air-conditioning, off-street parking, bicycles on request, dinner at extra charge with advance notice for groups of six or more, fishing and canoeing available nearby.

Rates: $$$. Visa, MasterCard, and personal checks.

Restrictions: No children under eight, no pets, restricted smoking.

Appomattox Manor Plantation

Hopewell, Virginia

From June 1864 until the end of the war, General Grant made his headquarters in this cabin on the lawn of Appomattox Manor Plantation, near the junction of the James and Appomattox Rivers. City Point became the center of the Union war effort during the Petersburg Campaign, and tents and cabins occupied nearly every available square foot of the plantation grounds. While Lee and his army suffered in the trenches before Petersburg, shiploads of food and supplies arrived daily for the Union forces. A special twenty-one-mile railroad was built and eighteen supply trains sped supplies to the front. The matériel pouring into City Point were a symbol of the Union's great advantage in the war—it simply had more than enough of everything. President Lincoln visited City Point on two occasions, using the drawing room of Appomattox Manor as his office. He was here for two of the last three weeks of his life. His ship, the *River Queen*, was moored just offshore. A day after Lincoln left, Grant moved closer to the Petersburg front and began his final offensive.

Appomattox Manor Plantation, at the intersection of Cedar Lane and Pecan Ave., is now the **City Point Unit of Petersburg National Battlefield** (see page 95). Two rooms at the Manor are open to the public, and General Grant's cabin still stands on the grounds. A fifteen-minute video is available, and visitors can take a self-guided walking tour. Open daily, 8:30–4:30, except for federal holidays. Admission is free. For information phone 804-458-9504.

Lynchburg Mansion Inn

Lynchburg, Virginia

Lee's tattered army was headed for the railroad here at Lynchburg when it was cut off by Grant and forced to surrender at Appomattox, a half-hour's drive away.

For a time before the war, Lynchburg was the second wealthiest city in America, and while the city has more than its share of grand mansions, none is grander than this one, once the home of self-made multimillionaire James R. Gilliam.

The beautiful columned house blends Spanish and Georgian elements, and each of its many rooms is a showcase. A large grand hall, with high ceilings and paneled wainscoting, opens onto a parlor furnished with Victorian antiques.

Innkeepers Bob and Mauranna Sherman have made sure that the guest rooms and suites are equally splendid. One of the suites opens onto a circular balcony. Morning begins with coffee and juice and a newspaper on a silver tray by your guest room door, a prelude to a gourmet breakfast that will see you through a morning of sightseeing.

Address: 405 Madison St., Lynchburg, VA 24504; tel: 804-528-5400 or 800-352-1195.

Accommodations: Five guest rooms, two of which are suites, all with private baths.

Amenities: Air-conditioning, off-street parking, fireplaces, hot tub on porch, library, garden with gazebo.

Rates: $$–$$$. All credit cards and personal checks.

Restrictions: No pets, no smoking.

NORTH CAROLINA

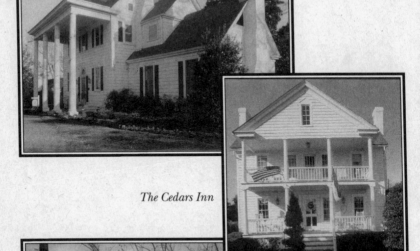

Arrowhead Inn

The Cedars Inn

Harmony House Inn

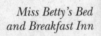

Miss Betty's Bed
and Breakfast Inn

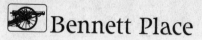 Bennett Place

Durham, North Carolina

Two old battle-weary adversaries, Joseph E. Johnston and William T. Sherman, met under a flag of truce midway between their lines on the Hillsborough Road, seven miles from Durham Station. Needing a place to confer, Johnston suggested a simple farmhouse a short distance away, the home of James and Nancy Bennett. The generals would meet here three times, struggling to achieve equitable terms of surrender. On April 26, 1865, the farmhouse became the site of the largest troop surrender of the war.

Striving to avoid capture in Virginia, President Jefferson Davis arrived in Greensboro, North Carolina, on April 11 and summoned Johnston to assess the strength of his army. Davis believed the South could and should continue the war, but the news of Lee's surrender prompted him to allow Johnston to confer with Sherman.

At their first meeting, Sherman showed Johnston a telegram announcing the assassination of Abraham Lincoln. Sherman explained that he was prepared to offer terms similar to those Grant gave Lee. Johnston demurred, saying he wanted "to arrange the terms of a permanent peace," political as well as military.

At the second meeting, on April 18, now knowing that Johnston's surrender wasn't a military necessity, Sherman gave Johnston a "memorandum or a basis of agreement." Johnston accepted the terms. This liberal document provided for an armistice that could be terminated on forty-eight hours' notice, and its provisions included the disbanding of Confederate armies following the deposit of arms in state arsenals, recognition of state government, establishment of federal courts, restoration of political and civil rights, and the promise of a general amnesty.

Davis, unhappy with the terms, ordered Johnston to disband his infantry and make an escape with the cavalry. Johnston, realizing the devastation a prolonged war would bring, disobeyed his president. He met with Sherman again at the farmhouse on April 26.

As it turned out, the final agreement was simply a military surrender ending the war in the Carolinas, Georgia, and Florida, affecting 89,270 Confederate soldiers. The mustering out of Johnston's troops and the issuing of pardons took place in nearby Greensboro.

Two more surrenders would follow. Richard Taylor surrendered his army in Alabama on May 4, and E. Kirby Smith surrendered his at Galveston on June 2. This meant that Confederate forces now were completely disbanded.

Bennett Place State Historic Site, 4409 Bennett Memorial Rd., Durham, NC 27705, is six miles west of Durham, then a half-mile south of I-85 on U.S. 70. From I-85 north, take Exit 170 onto U.S. 70, then, after approximately a half mile, turn right onto Bennett Memorial Rd. The site is a half mile farther on the right. From I-85 south, take Exit 173 and follow the signs.

The original buildings, destroyed by fire in 1921, have been reconstructed from wartime photographs and sketches. An audiovisual program tells of the Bennett family and the events that happened here.

Open April through October, daily, 9:00–5:00; November through March, daily except Monday, 10:00–4:00. Closed Thanksgiving and December 14–26. The surrender is re-enacted the first Sunday in December. Admission is free. For information phone 919-383-4345.

Bentonville Battleground

Newton Grove, North Carolina

It was the Confederacy's last chance to prevent General William Tecumseh Sherman's army, marching north from Georgia, from linking up with Grant, who had Lee's army pinned down at Petersburg. As Sherman's army entered North Carolina, hundreds of North Carolinians deserted Lee's army to protect their homesteads. General Joseph E. Johnston's small force had attempted to stem the tide at Aversboro on March 16, 1865, but the big battle, the biggest ever fought in the state, was here, three miles east of Newton Grove, on March 19, 20, and 21. It was the last battle in which a Confederate army was able to mount even a minor offensive.

With fewer than thirty thousand men, Johnston waited until miserable road conditions forced Sherman, who was headed for Goldsboro, to divide his sixty-thousand-man command into two wings. Discovering that the Union wings had become separated by a half-day's march, Johnston saw an opportunity to destroy first one wing, then the other. On the

evening of March 18, Johnston organized his forces into a
sickle-shaped line along the Goldsboro Road near the village
of Bentonville and waited. Sherman's left wing stumbled into
the trap. Initial attacks overran large sections of the Union
lines. But one division managed to hold on, despite being
attacked on both sides, and it saved the day. Failing to crush
the Union lines, Johnston pulled back to his original position.

Sherman's right wing arrived at the battlefield early the
next morning, and for two days cannon and rifle fire were
constant. On March 21 a force led by General Joseph A.
Mower outflanked the Confederate positions, coming within
two hundred yards of Johnston's headquarters before falling back. That evening the weary Confederates abandoned
their positions and withdrew north to Smithfield. Sherman
marched to Goldsboro, where supplies awaited him. More
than four thousand Union and Confederate troops were
killed, wounded, or missing during the battle at Bentonville,
fought in an area of six thousand acres.

The restored **Harper House** was used as a hospital for the
wounded of both sides. On the battlefield are original and
reconstructed trenches. An audiovisual show at the **Visitor
Center** explains the battle and its significance. The history
trail has markers and exhibits, and the roads in the area are
marked with plaques highlighting events of the battle.

Bentonville Battleground State Historic Site is fifteen
miles east of Dunn. From I-95, take Exit 90, drive fifteen miles
south on U.S. 701; turn left onto Rte. 1008, then drive three
miles east to the site. Besides the **Harper House** and the
trenches, there is a Confederate cemetery and a history trail
with exhibits. Open April through October, daily, 9:00–5:00,
Sunday 1:00–5:00; daily except Monday, 10:00–4:00, and
Sunday, 1:00–4:00, the rest of the year. Closed Thanksgiving
and December 24–26. Admission is free. For information
phone 910-594-0789.

Some forty miles north in Durham is the **Bennett Place
State Historic Site,** where, in April, Johnston surrendered his
army to Sherman.

Arrowhead Inn

Durham, North Carolina

This inn predates the Civil War; actually, it predates the Revolutionary War. The "Old House," as it was once called, was built between 1774 and 1780 by the Lipscomb family, who owned a two-thousand-acre plantation in the North Carolina Colony. It was on the "Great Path" over which Catawba and Waxhaw Indians traveled between Virginia and the mountains. Yankee soldiers also came this way during the war: a "boot" derringer of the type carried by many Union soldiers was unearthed on the premises recently. The Southern colonial manor house was lovingly restored before it became an inn in 1985. The guest rooms are all decorated in a tasteful interpretation of the Civil War period. A family (or a honeymoon couple) would enjoy the Land Grant Cabin. It has a sitting room with wood-burning fireplace, a sleeping loft, and a large bath.

The Arrowhead Inn feels as if it were blessedly far from everything, but it is only minutes away from Durham and the Bennett Place, where Johnston surrendered to Sherman. Stroll the four-acre grounds under 150-year-old magnolias; some thirty-three varieties of birds have been seen here. One of the innkeepers—Jerry, Barbara, or Cathy Ryan—is always on the premises to give directions or solve problems.

Address: 106 Mason Rd., Durham, NC 27712;
 tel: 919-477-8430 or 800-528-2207; fax: 919-471-9538.
Accommodations: Eight double rooms, all with private baths and phones.
Amenities: Gardens, birdwatching.
Rates: $$$. All major credit cards and personal checks.
Restrictions: No pets, but boarding kennel nearby; restricted smoking.

Miss Betty's Bed and Breakfast Inn

Wilson, North Carolina

An 1858 house, an Italianate "Painted Lady," is the head-quarters of this charming inn complex in the historic district of Wilson. The inn includes two historic houses, the Davis-Whitehead-Harris House and the adjacent Riley House.

The inn is on Nash Street, once described as one of the ten most beautiful streets in the country. Innkeepers Betty and Fred Spitz have given the inn period furnishings, and many of the antiques on display are museum quality (Betty is an antique dealer, and Wilson is considered the antique capital of the state).

The town's Maplewood Cemetery is the resting place of the Betsy Ross of the Confederacy, Rebecca M. Winbonne, who reportedly made the original Stars and Bars. Wilson is within easy driving distance of the Bentonville Battlefield in Newton Grove and the CSS *Neuse* State Historic Site in Kinston.

Address: 600 W. Nash St., Wilson, NC 27893; tel: 919-243-4447 or 800-258-2058.

Accommodations: Fourteen double rooms, all with private baths.

Amenities: Air-conditioning, off-street parking, fireplaces; phones and TVs in guest rooms, golf and tennis nearby.

Rates: $ single; $$ double, including full breakfast. All major credit cards and personal checks.

Restrictions: No children under thirteen, no pets, no smoking.

The Cedars Inn

Beaufort, North Carolina

This town (pronounced Bow-furt, unlike its South Carolina namesake Bew-furt) was settled in 1709, and is one of the oldest towns in the state. Federal forces occupied Beaufort in March 1862, and for the duration of the war it served as an important base of operations for the Union offensive in the South. The huge Federal fleet that delivered the death blow to the Confederacy in January 1865 assembled here.

Today Beaufort is a charming fishing village, and the houses in the historic district show the influence of trade with the West Indies. The Cedars, built about 1768, has been beautifully restored by innkeepers Sam and Linda Dark. They purchased the matching house next door, enabling them to double the number of guest rooms, and added a restaurant that is the best in town. The inn is on the waterfront in the historic district, a short walk from the interesting maritime museum and the other attractions of the town.

Address: 305 Front St., Beaufort, NC 28516; tel: 919-728-7036; fax: 919-728-1685.
Accommodations: Eleven double rooms, all with private baths.
Amenities: Air-conditioning, off-street parking, ferry service to offshore islands, bicycling, full breakfast in dining room.
Rates: $$–$$$. American Express, Visa, MasterCard, Discover, and personal checks.
Restrictions: No children under ten, no pets, restricted smoking.

Fort Macon

Atlantic Beach, North Carolina

Designed by General Simon Bernard, a French military engineer, to protect the Beaufort Inlet, Fort Macon was one of a chain of forts built along the Atlantic Coast after the War of 1812. Not long after it was garrisoned in 1834, it developed a problem with erosion. The army sent a young engineer to remedy the problem—Captain Robert E. Lee. The system of stone jetties he designed can be seen today.

Captured by the Confederates in 1861, it was recaptured a year later by a Union sea and land assault commanded by John G. Parke and Ambrose Burnside. After eleven hours of bombardment, commander Moses J. White surrendered the fort. Shells from Federal batteries firing rifled cannon had penetrated rooms near the powder magazine, creating the danger of a lethal explosion.

For the duration of the war, Fort Macon was under Union

control. It was used as a prison and a coaling station. The fort remained active until after World War II. An unusual accident occurred here in 1942. Soldiers found that the quarters in the fort were heated only by fireplaces. Civil War shells being used as andirons exploded, killing two soldiers and wounding several others.

Fort Macon is one of the best-preserved forts in the country. The outer and inner walls are separated by a deep, twenty-five-foot-wide moat. The outer walls are more than twenty feet thick, and allow magnificent views of the Beaufort Inlet. Twenty-six casements (vaulted rooms) are situated around the parade grounds, and some have been restored to represent the quarters of officers and men.

Fort Macon State Park is reached from I-40 or I-95. Take Rte. 70 east to Morehead City, turn onto the Atlantic Beach Bridge and follow right to the intersection with Rte. 58, turn left onto 58, and the park is at the end of the road. Open daily, 9:00–5:30. Closed Christmas. Museum in casement. Guided tours daily from Memorial Day to Labor Day. Civil War reenactments are held on the parade grounds on three summer weekends. West of the fort a park road leads to picnic grounds, a bathhouse and pavilion, and a public beach. Admission to fort and beach is free. For information phone 919-726-3775.

Harmony House Inn

New Bern, North Carolina

When you enter this handsome inn in the historic district, you will see framed prints from *Harper's Weekly* that depict the Battle of New Bern. The town fell to Union forces in March 1862, and served as their base of operations in eastern North Carolina for the rest of the war. This house was occupied by Company K of the Forty-fifth Massachusetts Regiment. A photograph of soldiers posing in front of the house may be seen in the inn.

Ed and Sooki Kirkpatrick bought Harmony House in 1994 and have refurbished the interior. Canopy beds and comforters grace the bedrooms, two new suites have been added, one with a heart-shaped Jacuzzi, and guests will enjoy the homemade decorations crafted by Sooki. The inn is on the National Register of Historic Places. The **Civil War Museum,** just down Pollock Street from the inn, displays one of the finest and most comprehensive private collections of Civil War firearms and accoutrements in the country. The museum, which is closed in the winter, will direct you to the houses in town that played a role in the war, although most are now private homes.

Address: 215 Pollock St., New Bern, NC 28560;
  tel: 919-636-3810 or 800-636-3113;
  E-mail: harmony@nternet.net.
Accommodations: Eight double rooms and two suites, all with private baths and phones.
Amenities: Air-conditioning, off-street parking, TV in rooms.
Rates: $$–$$$. Visa, MasterCard, Discover, and personal checks.
Restrictions: No pets, no smoking.

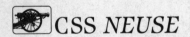CSS *NEUSE*

Kinston, North Carolina

After Federal troops occupied New Bern, the Confederate navy decided to build an ironclad gunboat on the Neuse River, take it downstream, and recapture the city. Pine forests would provide the lumber, and the shipwrights would be the local carpenters. Construction began in the fall of 1862, but was interrupted by a Federal raid in the area. The hull of the twin-screw ironclad steamer measured 158 feet long and 34 feet wide, and resembled a flat-bottomed river barge. Commissioned the CSS *Neuse*, it was launched in 1863 and floated down the river to Kinston, where it was to be fitted with machinery, guns, and iron armor plating. Problems delayed completion, and, in fact, the *Neuse* never did receive all its armor.

While steaming to New Bern it ran aground, and when the river rose it returned to Kinston, where it sat idle for ten months. As Federal troops approached in March 1865, Commander Joseph Price ordered the vessel scuttled in the river to avoid capture. While the *Neuse* never saw battle, its presence was an important factor in preventing Union forces from moving from New Bern to Goldsboro. The *Neuse* remained at the bottom of the river for nearly a century. It was raised in 1963 and moved here a year later. It's one of only three Civil War ironclads extant.

The **CSS *Neuse* State Historic Site** is near the city limits of Kinston. From I-95 take the Smithfield/Selma, NC, exit, then U.S. 70A east about forty-five miles to Kinston, then U.S. 70A to site. The wooden skeleton of the ironclad is on display. In the **Visitor Center,** an audiovisual presentation tells the story of the *Neuse* and has related exhibits and demonstrations of nautical blacksmithing. Historic photographs and artifacts are on display. Open April through October, daily, 9:00–5:00, Sunday 1:00–5:00; daily except Monday, 10:00–4:00, Sunday, 1:00–4:00, the rest of the year. Closed Thanksgiving, December 24–26, and other major state holidays. Admission is free. For information phone 919-522-2091.

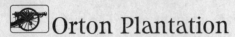

Orton Plantation
Wilmington, North Carolina

This magnificent mansion overlooking Cape Fear was built around 1730 and became the center of a large rice plantation. During the Civil War, Orton was used as a military hospital and was not destroyed, as many of the houses in the area were. The war left the owner, Thomas Miller, bankrupt, and the estate was abandoned until the 1880s, when it was bought and restored by former Confederate colonel Kenneth M. Murchinson.

Today the Orton Plantation is well known for its beautiful gardens with live oaks, magnolias, and ornamental plants. The old rice fields are now a wildlife refuge. In the spring, when the azaleas are in bloom, visitors come from all over the world.

Orton Plantation Gardens, eighteen miles south of Wilmington on NC 133. Grounds open March through November, daily except some holidays (mansion not open to public), 10:00–5:00. Admission is $8 for adults, $7 for seniors, and $3 for children two to twelve. For information phone 910-371-6851.

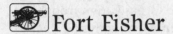

Fort Fisher

Kure Beach, North Carolina

By the last year of the war, Fort Fisher was a bone in the Union's throat. The huge earthwork fort at the mouth of the Cape Fear River kept the port of Wilmington open, allowing blockade runners to bring supplies for Lee's beleaguered army. Lee warned: "If Fort Fisher falls, I will have to evacuate Richmond."

The fort's forty-seven big guns threatened Federal warships trying to enforce the blockade, and its earth and sand mound construction readily absorbed shot and shell. Perched on a bluff, the fort was manned by two thousand troops.

In December 1864 Union warships bombarded Fort Fisher for two days without success. During a second attack, in January 1865, gunboats pounded the fort as Union troops stormed across the beach under intense fire, suffering heavy casualties. A large Union force, attacking from another side, found that the bombardment had blown a hole in the wall, entered, and captured the fort in bitter fighting.

The remaining forts in the Cape Fear area were evacuated, and when Union troops entered Wilmington, Lee's supply line was severed. The fall of the Confederacy was only a few months away.

The L-shaped fort was massive; the wall facing the sea was more than a mile long, the land wall a third of that. The earthwork walls rose twenty feet above the sea. To cushion the fort from naval gunfire, the walls were twenty-five feet thick.

Today erosion is slowly destroying Fort Fisher. All that is left are contoured mounds. In the small museum at the **Visitor Center** is a model of the fort in its glory years. Also on display are a reconstructed gun emplacement and items recovered from sunken blockade runners. An audiovisual program tells the story of the fort. An interpretive program is given in the summer, and a commemorative anniversary program is held at the fort in January.

Fort Fisher State Historic Site is open April through October, daily, and daily except Monday from November through March. Closed Thanksgiving and December 24–25. Admission is free. From Wilmington, take U.S. 421 south approximately twenty miles to Kure Beach. Fort Fisher is four miles past Kure Beach. A car ferry links the fort and Southport, a favorite of yachtsmen traveling the Intercoastal

Waterway. The ride takes about thirty minutes. For information phone 910-458-5538.

Go fourteen miles north of Southport on NC 133, then follow signs from the highway to **Brunswick Town-Fort Anderson State Historic Site,** 8884 St. Philips Rd. SE, Winnabow, NC 28479. The town was built by colonists during the 1720s. Across part of the site are the Civil War earthworks of Fort Anderson. The **Visitor Center** has exhibits and an audiovisual presentation. A Civil War encampment is held here in mid-February. Open April through October, daily; November through March, daily except Monday. For information phone 910-371-6613.

SOUTH CAROLINA

Bay Street Inn

Maison DuPre

Two Meeting Street Inn

The Chesnut Cottage

Greenleaf Inn

Bay Street Inn

Beaufort, South Carolina

When the Union fleet appeared, the people of Beaufort took flight. On the front steps of the Bay Street Inn are cracks where trunks were thrown from the upper gallery. General Isaac Stevens occupied the lovely town on December 11, 1861, and to his astonishment found it deserted by the white residents and looted by the freed slaves. Later the town became a rest and recuperation center for Union soldiers and sailors, the mansions used as hospitals, quarters for officers, and commissaries.

This house, built in 1852 by a cotton planter, became a hospital. It is a fine example of Southern Greek revival architecture, and among its defining features are fourteen-foot ceilings, a two-story veranda, and marble fireplaces. Many of the guest rooms have unobstructed water views. Host Peter Steciak likes to point out the inn's lovely gardens; the story goes that somewhere on the grounds are poinsettias that were planted by Joel Poinsett himself when he visited the mansion before the war.

Address: 601 Bay St., Beaufort, SC 29902; tel: 803-522-0050; fax: 803-521-4086.

Accommodations: Nine rooms, all with private baths.

Amenities: Air-conditioning, off-street parking, phones and cable TV in rooms, wine and cheese at 6:00, afternoon tea, on Intercoastal Waterway, beaches and historic sights nearby.

Rates: $$$. All credit cards and personal checks.

Restrictions: No children under eight, no pets, no smoking.

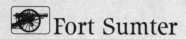

Fort Sumter

Charleston, South Carolina

I n retrospect, it seems inevitable that the war would have
started here. South Carolina was the first state to secede
from the Union, and no city in the South was more militant
than Charleston. The presence of a Federal fort in the harbor
was a constant irritant.

Jefferson Davis told General P. G. T. Beauregard to
order Major Robert Anderson to surrender the fort. When
Anderson refused, thirty guns and seventeen mortars from
shore batteries began to bombard the fort while the citizens
of Charleston looked on and cheered.

Thirty-four hours later, a fire in the fort raged out of control, threatening the powder magazine. Anderson was forced to surrender. That day, April 14, 1861, the Confederate flag flew over Fort Sumter.

This act of aggression prompted Lincoln to ask the states to send 75,000 troops to put down the rebellion. The South reacted by authorizing the enlistment of 100,000 for a year's service. The war had begun.

For most of the war, Fort Sumter was occupied by a Confederate garrison. During the siege of Charleston, 1863–65, more than half of the fort was demolished by Federal cannon fire.

Fort Sumter National Monument is on a man-made granite island in the harbor, four miles from downtown Charleston. Open daily except Christmas. Park Service tour boats leave from the City Marina on Lockwood Drive, just south of U.S. 17, and from the naval museum at Patriots Point in Mount Pleasant. During the summer there are three round-trips from each location. The trips cost $10 for adults, $9 for seniors and military personnel, and $5.50 for children six to twelve. For information phone 803-883-3123.

Charleston is a beautiful, aristocratic city where pastel-hued houses peek out from behind lacy iron gates. More than eight hundred of its buildings predate the Civil War. To capture the spirit of the city, see the multimedia presentation, *Charleston Adventures,* shown continuously at the **Visitor Center** in the Arch Building, 85 Calhoun St. For information phone 803-724-7474.

Among the prizes at the **Charleston Museum,** 360 Meeting St., is a full-size replica of the Confederate submarine *Hunley,* the first submarine to torpedo and sink a warship. Open Monday–Saturday, 9:00–5:00; Sunday, 1:00–5:00. For information phone 803-722-2996.

Charleston Walks, 334 E. Bay St., Suite 186, Charleston, SC 29401, offers two guided walking tours of particular interest. The Civil War Walk visits a slave market, the South Carolina Institute Hall, where the Ordinance of Secession was ratified, and the High Battery, from where rebel artillery fired on Fort Sumter. The other is the Low Country Ghost Tour, which visits cemeteries, houses, and other places where ghosts have been reported over the years. The tour, offered three times each evening, is sufficiently popular to have its own phone number: 803-853-GHOST. Each tour costs $12 for adults, $8 for children seven to fourteen, and no charge for children six and under.

Maison DuPre

Charleston, South Carolina

The people of Charleston gathered at the Battery in a party mood to cheer when the first shots of the war were fired at Fort Sumter in the harbor. The Battery is just a fifteen-minute walk from the Ansonborough District, where this delightful inn is located.

The Maison DuPre is made up of three restored homes and two carriage houses surrounding a charming courtyard. Two of the structures were moved to the site of this 1801 Federal house. The inn is owned by Robert and Lucille Mulholland and is managed by their son Mark.

The inn is furnished in period antiques, including the unique Charleston rice beds (stately four-posters with carvings of rice plants on each of the posts), and the decoration of each guest room is keyed to one of Lucille's paintings. An elegant Low Country tea is served every afternoon with sandwiches, cheeses, cakes, and cookies. Beds are turned down nightly and a chocolate left on the pillow. The staff will book dinner reservations, carriage rides, and tours.

Address: 317 E. Bay St., Charleston, SC 29401;
   tel: 803-723-8691 or 800-844-INNS; fax: 803-723-3722.
Accommodations: Fifteen double rooms, all with private baths.

Amenities: Air-conditioning, off-street parking, afternoon tea, concierge service, nightly turndown.

Rates: $$$, including continental breakfast. Visa, MasterCard, and personal checks.

Restrictions: No pets, restricted smoking.

Two Meeting Street Inn
Charleston, South Carolina

Fort Sumter, a Federal fort in Charleston harbor, was a bone in the city's throat. Rather than allow it to be resupplied by Lincoln, Jefferson Davis ordered it seized. When the bombardment began, on April 12, 1861, Charlestonians gathered on the Battery to watch.

Where this inn now stands, at Meeting and South Battery Streets, would have been a perfect vantage point to view the attack. Looking across the small park, which now has a number of Civil War cannon and mortars, Fort Sumter is clearly visible in the distance.

This grand Queen Anne mansion, a wedding present from a wealthy merchant to his daughter, is filled with family antiques and Oriental rugs, and has Tiffany stained-glass windows and intricately carved oak paneling throughout. The rocking chairs on the veranda provide a panoramic view of the Battery and the harbor.

Depending on the weather, the innkeepers, the Spell family, serve breakfast and afternoon tea in the formal dining room or on the veranda. Jean Spell is a licensed tour guide and points the way toward the historic places and pleasures of Charleston.

By any standards, Two Meeting Street is an exceptional inn, and a perfect complement to the Charleston experience.

Address: 2 Meeting Street, Charleston, SC 29401; tel: 843-723-7322.

Accommodations: Nine guest rooms, all with private baths.

Amenities: Air-conditioning, concierge service.

Rates: $$$, including continental breakfast and afternoon tea. Personal checks.

Restrictions: No children under twelve, no pets, restricted smoking.

🏛Greenleaf Inn

Camden, South Carolina

Camden was a Confederate storehouse and refugee center until General William T. Sherman's troops burned and looted most of it on February 24, 1865. In town when it happened, Mary Boykin Chesnut wrote in her diary: "All the railroads are destroyed, the bridges gone. We are cut off from the world, to eat out our own hearts."

Alice Boykin, a distant relative of the famous diarist, owns this charming inn. The inn is a compound composed of four buildings: the main inn, built in 1805; a carriage house (complete with carriage), built circa 1890; the McLaine house, built in 1890; and a guest cottage built in the 1940s. The guest rooms are decorated in the classic Victorian style and have four-poster beds, Oriental rugs, and period wallpaper.

Ms. Boykin will direct you to the little village of Boykin, about eight miles south of Camden on Rte. 261, where, in the Battle of Boykin Mill, badly outnumbered members of the South Carolina Home Guard made 2,500 Yankees pay dearly for coming this way. Among those killed in the battle was fifteen-year-old Burwell Boykin.

Address: 1308 Broad St., Camden, SC 29020; tel: 803-425-1806 or 800-437-5874; fax: 803-425-5853.

Accommodations: Eight double rooms, all with private baths, three suites, one cottage.

Amenities: Air-conditioning, ceiling fans, off-street parking, phones in rooms, use of nearby health club.
Rates: $$, including continental breakfast. All major credit cards and personal checks.
Restrictions: No pets, restricted smoking.

South Carolina State House
Columbia, South Carolina

The South Carolina State House is the only structure on Main Street that predates the burning of Columbia. When Sherman's army arrived outside the city on February 16, 1865, the general allowed that it was a "handsome granite structure." But when he saw the Confederate flag flying above it, he ordered his artillery batteries to fire on the building from across the Congaree River, a range of one mile. Bronze stars now mark the places where the shells hit.

Before continuing their march through the Carolinas, Sherman's men looted the state house, and in a mock session of the legislature repealed the Ordinance of Secession.

The **State House** may be toured Monday–Friday, 9:00–12:00 and 1:30–4:00. From I-26, which becomes Elmwood Ave., turn right onto Main St., which dead-ends at the statehouse at Gervais St. Several Civil War monuments are on the grounds. For information phone 803-734-9818.

Near the campus of the University of South Carolina is the **South Carolina Confederate Relic Room and Museum,** 920 Sumter St., where relics include firearms made in South Carolina, sabers, flags, currency, newspapers, photographs, and uniforms. Open Monday–Friday, 9:00–5:00. Admission is free. For information phone 803-734-9813.

On Garner's Ferry Road is **Millwood,** once the home of Wade Hampton II and of his son, the Confederate general

Wade Hampton III. The mansion was destroyed by fire during Sherman's occupation of Columbia. Only five front columns on brick bases remain of the Greek revival plantation home. Open dawn to dusk; reservations are suggested. Admission is free. For information phone 803-252-7742.

The Chesnut Cottage

Columbia, South Carolina

To read the diary entries of Mary Boykin Chesnut is to virtually enter the inner circle of the Confederacy. Her husband, James Chesnut, a prominent South Carolina lawyer and wealthy plantation owner, became an aide to Jefferson Davis, and the Chesnuts became part of the social elite in wartime Richmond. Mrs. Chesnut, a gifted writer and born gossip, saw it all and told it all. Excerpts from her diary have been published several times, from 1905 to the present. *Mary Chesnut's Civil War*, edited by C. Van Woodward and published in 1981, was awarded the Pulitzer Prize.

This house was the Chesnuts' temporary home during part of the war. President Davis stayed with them here in October 1864, and gave a speech from the front steps, a copy of which is on the night tables in the guest rooms. The house, built around 1850, is on the National Register.

The Mary Boykin Chesnut Room is feminine and has a queen-size canopy bed, while the masculine James Chesnut Room features an antique bed and Civil War memorabilia. The owner, Gale Garrett, is a genial host and serves a Southern breakfast worthy of Mrs. Chesnut herself.

Address: 1718 Hampton St., Columbia, SC 29210; tel: 803-256-1718.

Accommodations: Three double rooms in the cottage, and two suites in the carriage house, all with private baths (three have Jacuzzis).

Amenities: Air-conditioning, off-street parking, house tour by appointment.

Rates: $$.

Restrictions: Children at host's discretion, no pets, no smoking.

TENNESSEE

*English Manor
Inn*

Hilltop House

*Clardy's
Guest House*

Magnolia Manor

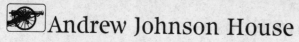Andrew Johnson House

Greenville, Tennessee

A tailor by trade, Andrew Johnson had little formal schooling. His wife read aloud to him while he sewed in his shop and spent her evenings teaching him to read. Johnson was a gifted debater and found his true calling in politics, rising from mayor of Greenville to governor of Tennessee to U.S. Senator.

Devoted to the Union, he remained in the Senate despite Tennessee's secession. Lincoln chose him as his running mate in 1864 and he became president after Lincoln was assassinated. Considered a traitor by Southerners and distrusted by many Northerners, he was determined to give the South the same generous terms as Lincoln had intended, but Congress had other ideas. Johnson was accused of wrongdoing, and at his impeachment trial in the Senate he missed being convicted by a single vote.

At the **Andrew Johnson National Historic Site,** Depot and College Sts., Greenville, TN 37744, are two homes, Johnson's tailor shop, and a museum, which displays mementos of his life, including a wedding coat he made. **The Homestead,** on Main St. between Summer and McKee Sts., was Johnson's home from 1851 to his death in 1875. The site is open daily, 9:00–5:00, except Thanksgiving, Christmas, and New Year's Day. Admission to **Visitor Center** and gravesite is free; Homestead tour is $2, free to seniors and youths seventeen and under. For information phone 423-638-3551.

🏛 Hilltop House

Greenville, Tennessee

On a hill overlooking the Nolichucky River Valley, Denise Ashworth, an English lady who made a career as a horticulturist and landscape architect in the National Forest Service, has turned a manor house, built in the 1920s, into a comfortable and charming inn.

All three guest rooms look out on the Appalachian Mountains, and two have their own verandas. Ms. Ashworth has furnished the house with English antiques, tasteful reproduction pieces, and Oriental rugs.

Including a visit to the nearby Andrew Johnson home, there is a lot to do around here: take a scenic drive, play a public nine-hole golf course, go white-water rafting, birdwatch or fish for trout in the National Forest, and hunt pheasant and quail in the local hunting preserve. Or you can just sit in a rocking chair on the front porch and enjoy the view.

In late October, the Battle of Blue Springs, a Confederate attempt in October 1863 to drive a Federal force out of East Tennessee, is reenacted nearby.

Address: #6 Sanford Circle, Greenville, TN 37743; tel: 423-639-8202.
Accommodations: Three double rooms, all with private baths.
Amenities: Air-conditioning, parking, small refrigerator upstairs for guests, afternoon tea, dinner by reservation and picnic baskets (both at extra cost).
Rates: $$, including full breakfast. American Express, Visa, MasterCard, and personal checks.
Restrictions: No children under three, no pets, no smoking.

Carter House

Franklin, Tennessee

On November 30, 1864, the Battle of Franklin was fought on the southern edge of this central Tennessee town. General John Bell Hood planned to march from Alabama through Tennessee into Kentucky, where he hoped to pick up recruits, defeat the Federal forces there, then go to Virginia to join Lee.

The first step in Hood's grand plan was to capture Nashville. Federal troops, commanded by General John M. Schofield, were dug in across the Columbia Pike here, south of Nashville, when Hood, over the objections of his officers, ordered a frontal assault.

In the late afternoon, 22,000 rebels marched across an open field, banners flying. Fierce hand-to-hand fighting up and down the line continued until well after dark. Sometime after midnight, Schofield withdrew his troops, but it hardly was a Confederate victory. Hood lost more than six thousand men, including twelve generals (five had been killed outright, one had been captured, and six more were wounded, one fatally) and more than half of his regimental commanders. Federal casualties were 2,300.

Some of the heaviest fighting swirled around this house, located just behind the Federal breastworks. As the battle raged through the night, the Carter family and their servants huddled in the cellar of the small brick home. When they emerged they learned that a son, Captain Tod Carter, lay wounded on the field. His father and sisters found him a few hundred yards from the house, and carried him home to die. The restored house is furnished with family heirlooms and period antiques.

The **Carter House,** 1140 Columbia Ave. (Rte. 31S), is open April through October, Monday–Saturday, 9:00–5:00, Sunday, 1:00–5:00; November through March, Monday–Saturday, 9:00–4:00, Sunday, 1:00–4:00. Admission is $6 for adults, $5 for seniors, and $2 for children twelve and under.

From I-65 take Exit 65, then Rte. 96 into town. At Court-house Square turn left on Main St., then left on Columbia Ave. The entrance is off Fowlkes St. For information phone 615-791-1861.

Carnton Mansion

Franklin, Tennessee

The Battle of Franklin was fought the night of November 30, 1864, and in only five hours of fighting, more Confederate soldiers were lost than in Pickett's Charge at Gettysburg. After the battle, the bodies of five generals were picked up and laid out on the back porch of this mansion, which was on the southern part of the battlefield.

The wounded began arriving in the early evening. Carpets were rolled back, furniture moved aside, and upward of two hundred wounded Confederate soldiers were crowded in. Hundreds more were cared for on the lawn. Doctors worked through the night, dressing wounds and amputating shattered arms and legs. This twenty-two-room mansion was built by Randall McGavock, a former mayor of Nashville, and the plantation was famous for its formal gardens and fine thoroughbreds. Sam Houston and James K. Polk were among the celebrities entertained here. The house, still in the process of being restored, is furnished with period pieces and McGavock heirlooms. The nearby family cemetery holds the graves of 1,481 Confederate soldiers.

Carnton Mansion, one mile southeast of Franklin off Rte. 431, is open January through March, Monday–Friday, 9:00–4:00; April through December, Monday–Saturday, 9:00–4:00, and Sunday, 10:00–4:00. Admission is $5 for adults, $4 for seniors, and $1 for children. Museum. Gift shop. For information phone 615-794-0903.

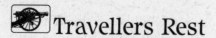

Travellers Rest

Nashville, Tennessee

For two weeks before the Battle of Nashville (December 15–16, 1864), a plantation house called Travellers Rest was the headquarters of John Bell Hood, the Confederate commander.

Riding from Murfreesboro to confer with Hood, Nathan Bedford Forrest spent the night here on December 11, 1864. During the battle, Federal forces charged the Confederate right flank on Peach Orchard Hill, within sight of the house.

The house was also the scene of several charges of the U.S. Colored Infantry. Several women and children were in the house during the fighting, but no one was injured. During the occupation of Nashville, Union troops camped on the grounds of the house.

Travellers Rest was built in 1799 for Judge John Overton, a friend of Andrew Jackson and a strong influence on his political career. The house has been restored to the period of Overton's residence, and the grounds contain a small museum.

Travellers Rest Historic House Museum, 636 Farrell Pkwy., Nashville, TN 37220, is open year-round, Tuesday–Saturday, 10:00–5:00; Sunday, 1:00–5:00. Admission is $6 for adults, $3 for children six to twelve. From I-65 take Harding exit, turn left onto Franklin Rd., go one mile, turn left onto Farrell Rd., then turn right onto Farrell Pkwy. For information phone 615-832-8197.

The **State Capitol,** 7th and Charlotte Aves., was completed in 1859, just in time to be swept up in the war. The fortifications around the Greek revival building consisted of four earthworks connected by a stockade with rifle loopholes. On the grounds is a statue of Sam Davis, a young hero of the Confederacy. Open weekdays, 8:00–5:00, Saturday, 9:00–4:00, Sunday, 10:00–4:00, except major holidays. For information phone 615-741-1621.

In the nearby James K. Polk State Building is the **Tennessee State Museum,** 5th and Deaderick, which has an extensive exhibit on the Civil War. Open daily except Monday and major holidays, 10:00–5:00, Sunday, 1:00–5:00. Admission is free. For information phone 615-741-2692.

English Manor Inn

Brentwood, Tennessee

The Battle of Nashville was a decisive point of the war. After losing Atlanta to Sherman, John Bell Hood moved north, hoping to reclaim this strategic city. But the Confederacy's last great offensive cost Hood his army.

The battle left a number of historic sites in the area, and a good place to make your headquarters while you explore them is in the suburb of Brentwood, where Willa "Deanie" English has turned her elegant colonial home on five wooded acres into a comfortable inn.

A friendly collie greets guests as they drive up, and a horse may be watching from the hill behind the columned house. Prepare to be pampered, from a comfortable bed in one of the handsome guest rooms to a hearty Southern breakfast to start the day right. Deanie is a caterer and will prepare picnic baskets or, with notice, dinner in the inn for guests too tired to go to one of the nearby restaurants.

Address: 6304 Murray Lane, Brentwood, TN 37027;
 tel: 615-373-4627; fax: 615-221-9666.
Accommodations: Seven guest rooms, all with private baths.
Amenities: Air-conditioning, off-street parking, phones in
 rooms, large-screen cable TV, picnic baskets and dinner on
 request (extra charge).
Rates: $$–$$$. All credit cards and personal checks.
Restrictions: No pets, restricted smoking.

Sam Davis Home

Smyrna, Tennessee

Sam Davis was the Nathan Hale of the Confederacy. The oldest of nine children, he enlisted and was wounded at Shiloh and again at Perryville. He was assigned to Coleman's Scouts, and in November 1863 was captured by Union troops carrying papers addressed to Bragg that outlined Union plans. Offered his freedom if he revealed his source, Davis replied: "If I had a thousand lives to live, I would give them all gladly rather than betray a friend." The twenty-year-old Davis was hanged as a spy.

Sam Davis's boyhood home was built circa 1820, and the Davis family came here in the late 1840s. They raised cotton, wheat, and tobacco, and owned about fifty slaves. Many original Davis family pieces are in the house. Among the outbuildings that remain are the overseer's house, kitchen, smokehouse, and a three-hole privy. In the family burial grounds near the house, a monument marks Sam Davis's grave. A small museum displays Civil War and Davis family artifacts.

The Sam Davis House, 1399 Sam Davis Rd., Smyrna, TN 37167, is open June through August, Monday–Saturday, 9:00–5:00, and Sunday, 1:00–5:00; September through May, Monday–Saturday, 10:00–4:00, and Sunday, 1:00–4:00. Admission and house tour are $4 for adults, $3.50 for seniors, and $2.50 for children. From I-24 east take Exit 66B and go 5.5 miles to Sam Davis Rd. From I-24 west, take Exit 70 and go five miles to Sam Davis Rd. For information phone 615-459-2341.

Oaklands

Murfreesboro, Tennessee

Oaklands, one of the most elegant houses in central Tennessee, was the center of a 1,500-acre plantation. During the war both Federal and Confederate armies camped on the lawn, and in June 1862 Colonel William Duffield, commander of the Ninth Michigan Regiment, made the house his headquarters.

A month later, Nathan Bedford Forrest led a daring early morning raid on the unsuspecting Federals, routed them, and in the house accepted the surrender of Murfreesboro from the injured Duffield.

In December 1862, Jefferson Davis and his aide, Robert E. Lee's son "Rooney," stayed here while visiting troops in the area. Oaklands, listed on the National Register of Historic Places, is operated by the Oaklands Association.

Oaklands, 900 North Maney Ave., is open Tuesday–Saturday, 10:00–4:00, and Sunday, 1:00–4:00. Admission and a guided house tour are $4 for adults, $3 for seniors, and $2 for children. For information phone 615-893-0022.

Clardy's Guest House

Murfreesboro, Tennessee

Just outside this central Tennessee town, from December 31, 1862, to January 2, 1863, a Confederate army fought bravely but failed to halt the Federal advance on Chattanooga. The engagement was called the Battle of Stones River and cost ten thousand Confederate and thirteen thousand Union casualties.

After the battle, the Federal army, now in control of central Tennessee, built Fortress Rosecrans here, a huge earthen fortification that also served as a supply depot.

This area is rich in Civil War history, and this Richardson Romanesque-style mansion-turned-inn is a good place to stay. It is a splendid representation of the turn-of-the-century architectural style, with masonry arches and balustrades. When the house was being built, the owner, J. T. Rather, who dreaded fire, had giant firecrackers built into the walls, on the theory that a fire would touch off the firecrackers and the noise would wake the family in time to get out safely. The theory, happily, has never been put to a test.

Today Robert and Barbara Deaton are the hosts at the inn, and delight in showing guests the features of the house—stained-glass windows, ornate carved mantels and woodwork, and rooms tastefully furnished with period antiques.

Address: 435 E. Main St., Murfreesboro, TN 37222; tel: 615-893-6030; fax: 615-833-7701.
Accommodations: Three guest rooms, two with private baths.

Amenities: Air-conditioning, off-street parking, golf and tennis nearby.

Rates: $$, including continental breakfast. No credit cards but personal checks accepted.

Restrictions: No pets, restricted smoking.

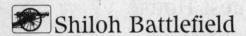Shiloh Battlefield

Shiloh, Tennessee

Ulysses S. Grant's forty-thousand-man Army of the Tennessee was camped near Pittsburg Landing, waiting for General Don Carlos Buell and his Army of the Ohio to arrive and join him in attacking the Confederate army at Corinth, Mississippi. Before Buell arrived, however, General Albert Sidney Johnston surprised Grant by attacking at dawn on April 6, 1862.

Although Johnston was mortally wounded later in the morning, the determined rebels pushed Grant back to the river and nearly captured the Union supply base at Pittsburg Landing. Buell's twenty-thousand-man army arrived in the night, however, and Grant counterattacked the second day, forcing the Confederates, now commanded by General P. G. T. Beauregard, to retreat toward Corinth.

Grant sent Sherman to try to catch the remnants of the rebel army, but ten miles out he ran into a rear guard commanded by Nathan Bedford Forrest, and decided to abandon the pursuit.

Shiloh, the first major battle in the West, was one of the fiercest in history. In two days, nearly 24,000 men were killed or wounded, or were missing in action. The Union casualty list shocked the nation. Veterans called it Bloody Shiloh. By failing to destroy Grant's army, the Confederates opened the way for him to attack Vicksburg.

Shiloh National Military Park is ten miles southwest of Savannah on TN 22. Open daily 8:00–5:00, except Christmas. Admission is $2 for adults, $4 for families. Guided tours are offered from Memorial Day to Labor Day. The **Visitor Center** has a small museum. For information phone 901-689-5275.

Magnolia Manor

Bolivar, Tennessee

Ulysses S. Grant made this house his headquarters on his way to Shiloh, and three of his generals—Sherman, Logan, and McPherson—also stayed here while their troops camped in a nearby walnut grove. Today, portraits of the four Union generals who stayed here hang in the entry hall.

Once Sherman made an ungracious comment about Southern women at dinner, and Grant ordered him to apologize. Later, in a fit of anger, Sherman took his saber and struck the banister, leaving a slash mark that is still visible.

The Georgian house was built in 1849 by Judge Austin Miller, a prominent lawyer and banker. Downstairs the ceilings are fourteen feet high and set off the museum-quality antique furnishings in the double parlor. Magnolia Manor is one of approximately twenty houses in the area that were spared by Union troops. Innkeepers Jim and Elaine Cox will arrange a tour of the historic district for guests. Shiloh is an hour's drive to the south.

Address: 418 N. Main St., Bolivar, TN 38008; tel: 901-658-6700; fax: 901-658-6700.

Accommodations: Two suites, one with private bath, and two double rooms that share a bath.

Amenities: Air-conditioning, off-street parking, VCR and cable TV in common room, restaurant on premises by reservation only, public golf and tennis nearby.

Rates: $$, including full breakfast. Personal checks (no credit cards accepted).

Restrictions: No children under twelve, no pets, restricted smoking.

GEORGIA

Gordon-Lee Mansion

The Whitlock Inn

The Veranda

Inn Scarlett's Footsteps

Maynard's Manor

The Manor House

1842 Inn

Chickamauga and Chattanooga Battlefields

Fort Oglethorpe, Georgia

The gateway to the heart of the Confederacy was Chattanooga, and to possess the city, two great armies clashed here in the fall of 1863 in some of the hardest fighting of the war.

Union general William S. Rosecrans had swept the Confederates from middle Tennessee and was determined to capture Chattanooga, but first he went southeast of the city to cut the rail line to Atlanta. Confederate general Braxton Bragg then abandoned Chattanooga and attempted to trap Rosecrans in northern Georgia. The armies met at Chickamauga.

On the first day, September 19, Bragg pushed the Union army back. The next day he tried in vain to drive between Rosecrans and Chattanooga, but couldn't crack the Union line. Then Bragg got lucky. A mistaken order opened a large gap in the Federal ranks. James Longstreet's troops smashed through, routing Rosecrans and half his army. General George H. Thomas took command and formed a new battle line on Snodgrass Hill, managing to hold it against repeated assaults. He earned the sobriquet, "Rock of Chickamauga."

At this crucial moment, if Bragg could have crushed Rosecrans's army before it could be reinforced, the war in the West would have turned out differently. His hesitation allowed the Union army to retreat into Chattanooga.

Bragg laid siege to the city. He occupied Missionary Ridge, Lookout Mountain, and the Chattanooga Valley. By placing artillery on the heights overlooking the river and blocking the roads and rail lines, Bragg prevented supplies from entering the city. Unless something was done quickly, Rosecrans's army would be starved into surrendering.

Reinforcements were sent. General Joseph Hooker arrived from Virginia with twenty thousand troops; Sherman brought sixteen thousand more from Mississippi. In October, General Ulysses S. Grant assumed overall command, replacing Rosecrans with General Thomas as commander of the Army of the Cumberland.

The situation soon began to change. Union troops opened a short supply route, called the "cracker line." Thomas attacked on November 23 and routed the Confederates from Orchard Knob. The next day, Hooker, aided by a heavy fog, pushed the Confederates out of their defenses around the Cravens House on Lookout Mountain. And the day after that, Sherman struck the right flank of Bragg's army concentrated on Missionary Ridge. Hooker attacked the rebel left.

The attack soon ran into trouble: Hooker was slow crossing Chattanooga Creek, and Sherman's attack couldn't crack the Confederate line. To take the pressure off Sherman, Grant ordered Thomas to attack the rifle pits at the base of Missionary Ridge.

Then something miraculous happened. Thomas's men spontaneously scaled the heights of Missionary Ridge in one of the great charges of the war. The rebel line collapsed, and Bragg's troops fled to the rear. During the night they retreated into Georgia.

The siege and battle for Chattanooga were over. Union armies now controlled the city and nearly all of Tennessee. Chattanooga became the base for Sherman's drive on Atlanta.

Chickamauga and Chattanooga National Military Park is composed of a number of separate areas, all of which can be toured easily in a day. The **Visitor Center,** located at the north entrance to the 5,400-acre Chickamauga battlefield, on U.S. 27, seven miles south of Chattanooga, is the best starting point. A seven-mile self-guided auto tour begins here. Rangers also give guided tours of the battlefield, evening programs, and summer musket- and cannon-firing demonstrations. The park is open daily, 8:00–4:45, to 5:45 in the summer. Closed Christmas. For information phone 706-866-9241.

🏛Gordon-Lee Mansion

Chickamauga, Georgia

This 1847 Greek revival house was the only structure in the village of Chickamauga to survive the battle. From September 16–19 it served as General Rosecrans's headquarters, then as his main hospital during the bloodiest two days in American history, when 37,000 men became casualties. With Rosecrans was his chief of staff, James A. Garfield, who later would become the twentieth president. After the Union army retreated into Chattanooga, twenty-five Confederate army doctors remained in the house, submitting to capture rather than leaving their patients.

The mansion, a National Historic Site, is now an inn, authentically restored and furnished in the period. The atmosphere of early Southern aristocracy is mirrored in the Oriental floor coverings, crystal and brass chandeliers, and ornate millwork. In the house are three guest rooms—the Red, Gold, and Blue rooms—all with their own baths, and a small apartment with a private entrance off the back veranda. Guests may also stay in a log house on the grounds.

Guests enjoy exploring the inn's seven manicured acres and its three gardens—a formal English garden, an herb garden, and a vegetable garden. They also enjoy the rocking chairs on the several verandas. An elegant but informal full Southern breakfast is served in the dining room.

The Gordon-Lee Mansion has it all. It is, in the author's opinion, the most outstanding Civil War inn in the country.

Address: 217 Cove Rd., Chickamauga, GA 30707;
tel: 706-375-4728; E-mail: GLMBB1@aol.com.
Accommodations: Four double rooms and a log house, all with private baths.
Amenities: Air-conditioning and cable TV in rooms, breakfast served in dining room.
Rates: $$, including full breakfast. Visa, MasterCard, and personal checks.
Restrictions: No children under twelve, except in log house, no pets, restricted smoking, two-night minimum in October and on weekends.

The Whitlock Inn

Marietta, Georgia

Here is an oasis of Victorian charm, a block away from the historic town square in Marietta, two miles from the Kennesaw battlefield, and eight miles from the Kennesaw Civil War Museum. On the way to the square (which has some good antique shops) you will pass the hotel where James J. Andrews, the Union spy, and his men stayed the night before they stole the train, the *General*.

The town has a number of antebellum homes, and innkeeper Alexis Edwards will give you a map and help you plan a walking tour of the historic district. The national cemetery here has ten thousand Union graves; the Confederate cemetery, three thousand.

The inn is a restored Victorian mansion with period furnishings and modern conveniences. The porch has comfortable rockers and the garden is a delight.

Address: 57 Whitlock Ave., Marietta, GA 30064; tel: 770-428-1495; fax: 770-919-9690.

Accommodations: Five guest rooms, all with private baths.

Amenities: Climate-control, off-street parking, phones and cable TV in rooms, public golf course nearby. Fax machine and copier available.

Rates: $$–$$$, including continental breakfast and afternoon snacks. Major credit cards and personal checks.

Restrictions: No children under twelve, innkeeper will make arrangements to board pets, no smoking.

The Kennesaw Civil War Museum

Kennesaw, Georgia

The star attraction here is one of the most celebrated relics of the war, the *General*, the steam locomotive whose theft by Union saboteurs led to the "Great Locomotive Chase."

On April 12, 1862, a band of twenty-two soldiers, dressed in civilian clothes and led by the spy James J. Andrews, boarded the train in Marietta. When the train stopped at Big Shanty, they uncoupled the passenger cars, commandeered the locomotive, and took off for Chattanooga, planning to destroy railroad bridges and tunnels along the way.

They were pursued by the irate conductor, who managed to find another locomotive and some volunteers for the chase. The *General* ran out of steam at the Tennessee border and the saboteurs were captured. Andrews and seven others were hanged, but the entire band was posthumously awarded Medals of Honor.

This incident was the inspiration for two motion pictures: the 1926 silent comedy *The General,* starring Buster Keaton, and Disney's 1966 *The Great Locomotive Chase,* starring Fess Parker.

The Kennesaw Civil War Museum, 2829 Cherokee St., Kennesaw, also displays a collection of Civil War artifacts. Open March through November, Monday–Saturday, 9:30–5:30, Sunday, 12:00–5:00; December through February, Monday–Saturday, 12:00–5:30, Sunday, 12:00–5:00. Admission is $3 for adults, $1.50 for children seven to fifteen. For information phone 770-427-2117.

The Atlanta Cyclorama

Atlanta, Georgia

In a special building in Grant Park is a giant painting-in-the-round that depicts "The Battle of Atlanta." It is forty-two feet high, 358 feet in circumference, weighs more than nine thousand pounds, and covers more than sixteen thousand square feet of canvas. In front of the canvas is a strip, called a diorama, containing a three-dimensional landscape with soldiers, horses, and other paraphernalia of war. Visitors sit in the center on a bleacher-like stand. When the lights go down and the narration and music begin, the stand slowly revolves, giving visitors the sensation that they are in the center of the great battle.

Cycloramas were popular entertainments in the years following the Civil War, but only this one and the one at Gettysburg survive. Elsewhere in the building is shown a film on the Atlanta Campaign, narrated by James Earl Jones. A small museum displays artifacts and mementos of the Battle of Atlanta. Nearby in the park are traces of a temporary Confederate fortification.

The **Cyclorama** is open daily, 9:20–4:30 in the fall and winter, 9:20–5:30 in the spring and summer. Bookstore. Admission is $5 for adults, $4 for seniors, and $3 for children six to twelve. From I-20 east, take Exit 26 and follow signs to park. The entrance to **Grant Park** is off Cherokee Avenue in southeast Atlanta. For information phone 404-658-7625 or 404-658-7626.

Ansley Inn
Atlanta, Georgia

Although this inn wasn't around when Atlanta was a battlefield, it is charming and friendly and located in one of the city's oldest and nicest neighborhoods, a short walk from such attractions as the High Museum, Piedmont Park, and the Woodruff Arts Center.

The turn-of-the-century Tudor mansion became an inn a decade ago, but retains many of its manoral touches. The living room, where afternoon drinks and appetizers are served, has a marble fireplace and easy chairs. Many of the furnishings in the house are original.

Address: 253 15th St. NE, Atlanta, GA 30309; tel: 404-872-9000 or 800-446-5416; fax: 404-892-2318.

Accommodations: Twelve double rooms in main house, six in annex, one of which is a two-room suite, all with private baths.

Amenities: Air-conditioning, off-street parking; phones, cable TV, whirlpool baths, and wet bars in rooms. Convenient to MARTA, local rapid transit to downtown Atlanta.

Rates: $$–$$$, including continental breakfast and afternoon refreshments.

Restrictions: No pets.

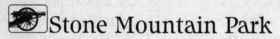Stone Mountain Park

Stone Mountain, Georgia

The centerpiece of this 3,200-acre family park is the largest piece of exposed granite in the world. It measures two miles in length, five miles in circumference, and 825 feet in height. General Sherman and his army passed this way on their famous March to the Sea. On the side of the monolith has been carved a spectacular 90-by-190-foot-high bas-relief sculpture of Jefferson Davis, Robert E. Lee, and Stonewall Jackson, each astride a horse. It took three sculptors more than fifty years to create this Confederate symbol; it was finally completed in 1970.

On summer nights, a fifty-minute laser show is projected on the north side of the mountain. A replica of a Civil War-era train makes the five-mile trip around the base. A cable car takes visitors to the top for a view of Atlanta, sixteen miles to the west. Athletic visitors enjoy hiking to the top.

Elsewhere in the park, the **Memorial Hall Museum** has excellent collections of Civil War weapons, uniforms, flags, and other memorabilia, and displays on local history. Nearby are nineteen antebellum buildings, all restored and authentically furnished, which were brought here from various places in Georgia to show visitors the working life of a plantation.

Visitors can ride around the park on a vintage steam passenger train, departing from a reproduction of Atlanta's

remarkable 1853 railroad station. The park has a thirty-six-hole golf course, a miniature golf course, ten miles of nature trails on twenty wooded acres, a 363-acre lake with a beach, cabana, fishing, boat rentals, and a scenic boat called the *Scarlett O'Hara*. There are three restaurants and countless snack bars. And in the summer, from Wednesday–Saturday, there are concerts by a 732-bell carillon.

Stone Mountain Park is open daily, 6:00 A.M. to midnight. Attractions are open daily, 10:00–5:30, 10:00–8:00 in the summer. Admission is free; $6 parking fee per car. From I-285 take Exit 30B (Hwy. 78), go seven miles east, and follow signs. The park is sixteen miles east of Atlanta. For further information phone 770-498-5702.

1842 Inn

Macon, Georgia

Jefferson Davis passed through here as he, his wife, and some of his cabinet members fled south in April 1865 to avoid capture. Earlier, this vital railroad center manufactured ordnance and quartermaster supplies for the Confederacy. Union forces were twice repulsed, but the city finally fell to Wilson's raiders on April 20, 1865.

Years later, when Jefferson Davis hosted a reunion ball in Macon for Confederate leaders, many dignitaries stayed at this inn. The inn was restored in 1986 and has won many preservation awards, and also many other awards for excellence, including the AAA's Four Diamond Award.

The white-pillared porch is lit at night to welcome guests, and the comfortable guest rooms have many amenities. Some of the guest rooms are in the adjacent Victorian cottage that shares a quaint courtyard and garden with the main house. The 1842 Inn is in the city's historic district.

Address: 353 College St., Macon, GA 32201; tel. and fax: 912-741-1842; reservations: 800-336-1842.

Accommodations: Twelve double rooms in the main house, nine in the cottage, all with private baths.

Amenities: Air-conditioning, off-street parking; phone, cable TV, and fresh flowers in rooms (some rooms have fireplaces and canopied beds); evening hors d'oeuvres in the library; dinner arrangements at a private club; tennis, swimming, and golf at affiliated country club; access to nearby health club.

Rates: $$–$$$, including continental breakfast. American Express, Visa, MasterCard, and personal checks.

Restrictions: No children under twelve, no pets, restricted smoking.

Robert Toombs House

Washington, Georgia

Outspoken and independent, Robert Toombs had a turbulent career as state legislator, congressman, and senator. A "founding father" of the Confederacy, he believed he should have been chosen president, not Jefferson Davis. He reluctantly accepted appointment as secretary of state, then resigned to be an officer in the Army of Northern Virginia. When his ambitions were frustrated, he resigned his commission and spent the remainder of the war years at his home in Washington, brooding and criticizing the Confederate government.

Federal troops came to the house to arrest him, but he escaped and fled the country. Returning home years later, he scorned the thought of accepting a pardon. In 1880 he boasted, "I am not loyal to the existing government of the United States and do not wish to be suspected of loyalty."

The house, built between 1797 and 1885, has been restored and has period furnishings, exhibits, and an excellent audiovisual program about Toombs's career.

The **Robert Toombs House State Historic Site,** 216 E. Robert Toombs Ave., Washington, GA 30673, is open Tuesday–Saturday, 9:00–5:00, and Sunday, 2:00–5:30. Closed Thanksgiving, Christmas, and New Year's Day. Admission is $2.50 for adults, $1.50 for children six to eighteen. For information phone 706-678-2226.

Maynard's Manor

Washington, Georgia

President Davis, his wife, and a number of Confederate leaders were fleeing south when they paused in this central Georgia town on May 5, 1865, to hold the last Confederate cabinet meeting. On June 4, Union soldiers arrested Davis near Irwinville, Georgia, and seized $100,000 of the $500,000 in gold taken from Richmond and last held in a bank here.

Legend has it that some of the gold is buried around here, and fortune hunters still ply the old stagecoach road looking for the lost fortune. Whether you're looking for Confederate gold or just Confederate sites, Maynard's Manor is a good place to make your headquarters. The Robert Toombs house is a short walk away, for example, and just east of town is the house of the old Mount Pleasant plantation, where Eli Whitney was employed as a tutor when he invented the cotton gin.

This Victorian cottage offers both comfort and privacy. Hosts Ross and Louise Maynard pamper guests with wine and hors d'oeuvres in the late afternoon, dessert after they return from dinner, and sherry, fruit, and flowers await in the comfortable rooms. Their gourmet breakfast is a delight, and they know what to see and do in the Washington area.

Address: 402 N. Alexander Ave., Washington, GA 30673; tel: 706-678-4303.
Accommodations: Three double rooms.
Amenities: Air-conditioning, off-street parking, TV.
Rates: $$–$$$. Visa, MasterCard, and personal checks.
Restrictions: No children, no pets, no smoking.

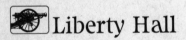 # Liberty Hall

Crawfordville, Georgia

Liberty Hall was the home of Alexander H. Stephens, the brilliant vice president of the Confederacy. He was sickly and weighed only ninety pounds but was said to have harbored sufficient "hostility and wrath . . . to burst ten thousand bottles."

As a congressman, Stephens opposed secession but bowed to the will of his fellow Georgians, and later reluctantly accepted the vice presidency. Stephens absented himself from the capital for long periods of time and, when he did assume his duties as presiding officer of the senate, used the office as a platform from which to attack President Davis and his conduct of the war.

Arrested by Federal troops and imprisoned at war's end, Stephens returned to Congress from 1873 to 1882, then was elected governor of Georgia.

A. H. Stephens State Historic Park, in Crawfordville, is reached from I-20; take Exit 55 and follow signs two miles to the park. The house contains Stephens's furniture and law library. The adjacent **Confederate Museum** displays Civil War weapons, uniforms, and artifacts. Open Tuesday–Saturday, 9:00–5:00, and Sunday 2:00–5:00; the last tour is at 4:00. Admission is $2.50 for adults, $1.50 for children five to eighteen. There are many other park facilities, for camping and sports. For information phone 706-456-2602.

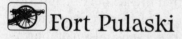

Fort Pulaski

Savannah, Georgia

This fort, a superb example of military architecture, was designed to protect the port of Savannah. It was considered invincible, "as strong as the Rocky Mountains," but it fell in thirty hours to a Union attack, a victim of new technology.

Construction began in 1829 and it took eighteen years, a million dollars, and twenty-five million bricks to complete. When war came, the unmanned fort was seized by Confederate troops, but they couldn't hold it for long. In 1861 Federal forces came ashore to prepare for siege operations. The

defenders felt safe. The Federal artillery was positioned on Tybee Island, at a range of one to two miles, more than twice the effective range of the heavy ordnance of that time.

The defenders were unaware that the artillery included ten new experimental rifled cannon, which soon were sending projectiles crashing through the fort's seven-and-a-half-foot-thick walls. Wide gaps were opened, and explosive shells passing through the holes threatened the powder magazine. Thirty hours after the bombardment began, the fort surrendered.

Fort Pulaski, on Cockspur Island, is located fifteen miles east of Savannah on U.S. 80; a causeway links the island to the mainland. Open daily, 8:30–5:00, except on Christmas. The **Visitor Center** contains a small museum and offers a fifteen-minute audiovisual presentation, lectures, weapon demonstrations, and guided tours by advance reservation. Admission is $2 for adults, children under sixteen free, maximum charge of $4 per car. For information phone 912-786-5787.

Green-Meldrim House
Savannah, Georgia

When William Tecumseh Sherman arrived in Savannah, he planned to make his headquarters in a hotel. Charles Green, a wealthy English cotton broker, offered him the use of his home. "If you don't take it," Green said, "some other general will. I much prefer you."

The house, now called the Green-Meldrim House, is one of the city's most striking, a blend of Georgian and Gothic revival styles with battlements and a cast-iron porch. Its rooms are filled with Italian sculpture and European paintings.

It was from this house that Sherman sent President Lincoln the telegram that read: "I beg to present to you, as a Christmas gift, the city of Savannah, with 150 heavy guns and plenty of ammunition; also, about 25,000 bales of cotton."

Green-Meldrim House, St. John's Church, 1 W. Macon St., Savannah, GA 31401, is now owned and operated by the St. John's Episcopal Church. Tours Tuesday, Thursday, Friday, and Saturday, 10:00–4:00. It is closed the two weeks before Easter, December 15–January 15, and the week of November 10. Admission is $4 for adults, $2 for students. For information phone 912-232-1251.

The Manor House
Savannah, Georgia

Built for the Lester Byrd family in the 1830s, this handsome Georgian house was used by Union officers in 1864, after Sherman and his army arrived in Savannah just in time for Christmas. Now an all-suite inn, it is tucked away in the residential part of the city's famed historic district, a short walk from the Green-Meldrim House where William Tecumseh Sherman made his headquarters after he marched through Georgia.

The Manor House is a luxurious town house. Each of the double parlors has a cozy fireplace, and all are furnished with fine English and American antiques. Oriental rugs grace polished heart-of-pine floors. Each guest suite has all the comforts of a luxury hotel—a gas fireplace in the comfortable sitting room, fresh flowers, milled soaps and bath salts, percale sheets, down-filled pillows, and a nightly turndown service with brandy and chocolates left by the bed.

Guests may choose to have breakfast, which comes with flowers and the morning paper, in their rooms or on their private verandas.

Address: 201 W. Liberty St., Savannah, GA 31401;
 tel: 912-233-9597 or 800-462-9597; fax: 912-236-9419.
Accommodations: Five suites with private baths.
Amenities: Climate-control, off-street parking; TV and VCR in
 rooms, some of which have whirlpool tubs. Private verandas.
 Honor bar in living room. Concierge service.
Rates: $$$, including continental breakfast and welcoming
 sherry.
Restrictions: No children under twelve, pets on first floor only,
 no smoking.

Inn Scarlett's Footsteps

Concord, Georgia

If *Gone with the Wind* is your favorite movie, you are going to love it here. K. C. and Vern Bassham bought this white-columned plantation house in 1993 and made it a bed-and-breakfast with a *GWTW* theme. Scarlett and Rhett would be right at home. The strains of *Tara's Theme* greet you when you approach the front door, which is framed by magnolias and live oaks.

The Basshams, who dress in period costumes, have assembled an impressive collection of *GWTW* memorabilia, and enjoy showing their prizes to guests. The inn is furnished in period antiques, and each bedroom is named for a different *GWTW* character.

A ball and a barbecue are held at Christmas, and a Civil War reenactment is a summer event.

Address: 40 Old Flat Shoals Rd., Concord, GA 30206; tel: 770-884-9012; E-mail: gwtw@gwtw.com.

Accommodations: Four double rooms, one suite, all with private baths; five cottages, all with TV and whirlpools, one especially for honeymooners.

Amenities: Cable TV and phone in library, *GWTW* museum, gift shop in carriage house, golf course five minutes away.

Rates: $$–$$$. American Express, Visa, MasterCard, and personal checks.

Restrictions: No children under ten, no pets, restricted smoking.

The Veranda
Senoia, Georgia

When it was built in 1906, this was a Victorian-style hotel called the Hollberg Hotel, and William Jennings Bryan, the three-time Democratic candidate for president, was one of the notables who stayed here.

For years it was host to the annual reunion of Georgia's Confederate Veterans, and a young reporter from the *Constitution* named Margaret Mitchell used to come down from Atlanta to listen to their stories, some of which found their way into a book she was writing called *Gone with the Wind*.

Everything about the place says relax, make yourself comfortable. No wonder the inn has built a loyal following among travelers. In the parlor are cozy rocking chairs and a rare 1930 Wurlitzer player piano-organ complete with chimes, and a collection of antique games and puzzles. The guest rooms have quilts and fresh flowers.

The hosts are Jan Boal, a college math professor, and his wife, Bobby, who has written several children's books.

Address: 252 Seavy St. (Box 177), Senoia, GA 30276;
  tel: 770-599-3905.
Accommodations: Nine double rooms, all with private baths.
Amenities: Air-conditioning, parking, gourmet evening meal
  available, gift shop.
Rates: $$$, including full breakfast. American Express, Visa,
  MasterCard, and Discover.
Restrictions: No pets, no smoking.

Andersonville Prison

Andersonville, Georgia

Disease and malnutrition killed men in every military prison, North and South, but this one was the worst. One prisoner described prison life at Andersonville in his diary: "There is so much filth about the camp that it is terrible trying to live here. With sunken eyes, blackened countenances from pitch pine smoke, rags and disease, the men look sickening. The air reeks with nastiness."

Nearly thirteen thousand Union soldiers perished here in fourteen months, and Andersonville became so notorious that its very name became a rallying cry for those who wanted to punish the Confederate States for leaving the Union. (The author's great-great-grandfather, Charles S. George, an eighteen-year-old private in the Twelfth Vermont Infantry, was

a prisoner at Andersonville for eleven months. When he enlisted he weighed 168 pounds; when he was released he weighed nearly half that, 88 pounds.)

When the war ended, the commandant, Captain Henry Wirz, was arrested and charged with "murder, in violation of the laws of war." Wirz was tried by a military tribunal as a war criminal, found guilty, and hanged.

Today Andersonville has a new role: it is a memorial to all Americans ever held as prisoners of war. On the site is a National Cemetery, the final resting place of the 12,912 prisoners who died here. The cemetery is hauntingly beautiful, and to wander among the white headstones is an emotional experience.

Andersonville National Historic Site is sixty-five miles south of Macon and ten miles northeast of Americus on GA 49. It is open daily, 8:00–5:00, except Christmas and New Year's Day. An audiotape to accompany the self-guided tour is available as well as an audiovisual presentation on the American Prisoner of War experience. On the last weekend in

February, the opening of the prison is reenacted, and on the first weekend in October there is a reenactment of the opening of the National Cemetery. Admission is free. For information phone 912-924-0343.

A Place Away Cottage Bed and Breakfast

Andersonville, Georgia

Guests coming here to learn about the notorious Confederate prison camp will find no better teacher than Peggy Sheppard, the owner of this rustic bed-and-breakfast. A former teacher in the local school system, she wrote a small book about the prison's history, *Andersonville, Georgia, USA*, and published it herself; it is now in its eleventh printing.

One of Ms. Sheppard's recent guests was a direct descendant of Captain Henry Wirz, the prison camp commander. The guest, Heinrich Wirz, a Swiss army colonel, was here to take part in a program to help create a better understanding of his unfortunate ancestor's role at the camp.

The cottage, built in 1923 to house the school principal, is a block away from the town's little Civil War Village, a collection of antique shops and restaurants, and a half-mile from the old prison. Ms. Sheppard personally delivers breakfast.

Address: 111 Oglethorpe St. (PO Box 26), Andersonville, GA 31711; tel: 912-924-1044 or 912-924-2558.
Accommodations: Two double rooms with private baths.
Amenities: Air-conditioning, fireplaces, ceiling fans and TV in each room. Refrigerator and coffee-maker.
Rates: $, including continental breakfast. No credit cards but personal checks accepted.
Restrictions: No pets.

ALABAMA

Plantation House Inn

Red Bluff Cottage

Malaga Inn

Grace Hall

First White House of the Confederacy

Montgomery, Alabama

This 1835 simple two-story white frame house was the residence of provisional president Jefferson Davis and his family during the three months that Montgomery was the capital of the Confederacy. In 1921 the house was moved from its original location at Bibb and Lee Streets to a site across from the state capitol. Now a Confederate museum, it contains period furnishings, Confederate mementos, and many personal belongings and paintings of the Davis family.

From I-85 take the Union St. exit, go four blocks to Washington St., and turn left. It is the first house on the left. The house, 644 Washington Ave., is open Monday–Friday, 8:00–4:30. Admission is free. For information phone 334-242-1861.

A bronze star between the columns of the **State Capitol,** 468 S. Perry St., marks the spot where Davis was inaugurated president of the Confederacy on February 18, 1861.

Plantation House Inn

Prattville, Alabama

Ten miles from the old Confederate capital of Montgomery is Prattville and the Plantation House Inn. It is an 1832 clapboard Greek revival house, tucked away among 150-year-old trees on land that was originally part of a grant from Andrew Jackson.

Some of Sherman's troops were active in this area but probably rode right by without seeing the house. Be careful or you'll do the same, and it would be a shame if you did. The house is old-timey, with huge bedrooms, nine fireplaces, and mahogany doors and moldings.

In 1989 the structure survived a devastating fire and was restored and updated by innkeepers John and Bernice Hughes, with a new kitchen and breakfast area.

Address: 752 Loder St., Prattville, AL 36067; tel: 295-361-0442.
Accommodations: Three rooms, one with private bath.
Amenities: Central air-conditioning, off-street parking, phones and cable TV in rooms, swimming pool.
Rates: $$, including full breakfast. No credit cards, but personal checks accepted.
Restrictions: Special arrangements for children under twelve necessary, no pets, no smoking.

Red Bluff Cottage

Montgomery, Alabama

Moving the Confederate capital to Richmond did not spare Montgomery from the ravages of war. Wilson's raiders entered the city on April 12, 1865, and retreating rebels burned the city's cotton stores. The raiders then demolished whatever industrial facilities might have served the South, leaving the city in shambles.

Some of the ancestors of the innkeepers, Mark and Anne Waldo, fought in the war, and some of their belongings may be seen in the inn today. The inn is a re-creation of a traditional Low Country Raised Cottage, furnished with antiques and period reproductions.

Local attractions, which the Waldos will direct you to, include St. John's Episcopal Church, where you will see the pew used by the Jefferson Davises; the Teague House, a mansion used as the headquarters for Union general James H. Wilson after his raiders occupied the city; and Old Alabama Town, a collection of historic structures, many of them dating from before the war.

Address: PO Box 1026, 551 Clay St., Montgomery, AL 36101; tel: 334-264-0056; fax: 334-263-3054; E-mail: RedblufBnB@aol.com.
Accommodations: Four double rooms, all with private baths.
Amenities: Air-conditioning, off-street parking.
Rates: $$. All major credit cards and personal checks.
Restrictions: No pets, no smoking.

Malaga Inn
Mobile, Alabama

The Confederacy seemed to be winning the war in 1862 when two merchants, who were brothers-in-law, built matching town houses next door to one another on a tree-lined street near Mobile Bay. Their fortunes took a turn for the worse when Admiral David Farragut steamed his fleet into the bay on August 5, 1864, shouting, "Damn the torpedoes! Full speed ahead!"

A century or so later, the houses were acquired by Mayme Sinclair, a local realtor, who joined the houses by adding a central entrance, patio, and garden to create the Malaga Inn, which she named for Mobile's sister city in Spain. The inn is now operated by Julie Beem. The rooms are furnished in period antiques; the restaurant, Mayme's, serves up delicious regional specialties; and the surrounding historical district invites strolling.

Address: 359 Church St., Mobile, AL 36602; tel: 334-438-4701 and 800-235-1586.
Accommodations: Thirty-eight double rooms and three suites.
Amenities: Air-conditioning, off-street parking, phones and TV in rooms, restaurant on premises, swimming pool.

Rates: $$. All major credit cards except Diners Club and personal checks.
Restrictions: No pets, restricted smoking.

Grace Hall

Selma, Alabama

B efore the war Selma had a plantation aristocracy second
to none. Planters vied to see who could build the grandest
mansion and breed the fastest thoroughbreds. During the war
it became a major Confederate munitions and manufacturing
center, and the Union army wanted to put it out of business.

On April 2, 1865, General James H. Wilson's raiders captured the city, and looted and burned it. The naval foundry,
rolling mill, powder works, and arsenal were destroyed.

Some antebellum mansions survived, however, including
Grace Hall, known locally as the 1857 Ware-Baker-Jones House
for the three families who lived here for more than 110 years.
Owners Coy and Joey Dillon restored the house and wandered
into the hospitality business when the mayor asked them to
put up a visiting dignitary.

The house has double parlors, a library with a pressed-tin
ceiling, heart-of-pine floors, ten-foot-tall windows, and brass
chandeliers. The bedrooms have marble fireplaces, carved
step-up rosewood beds, and enameled clocks.

Address: 506 Lauderdale St., Selma, AL 36701;
   tel: 334-875-5744; fax: 334-875-9967; E-mail: coyethelink.com.
Accommodations: Six double rooms, all with private baths.
Amenities: Air-conditioning, off-street parking, phones and
   cable TV in rooms, house tour.
Rates: $$. All credit cards and personal checks.
Restrictions: Pets by prior approval, restricted smoking.

MISSISSIPPI

Millsaps Buie House

Monmouth

Cedar Grove

Dunleith

The Mockingbird Inn

The General's Quarters

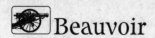Beauvoir

Biloxi, Mississippi

Jefferson Davis and his family spent the last ten years of his life at this estate on the Gulf of Mexico. After his release from imprisonment at Fort Monroe, Virginia, he accepted the offer of Mrs. Sarah Dorsey, a family friend, to stay at Beauvoir, so named for its beautiful view of the Gulf.

At first Davis stayed in a cottage on the grounds, then two years later he purchased the property and was joined by his wife, Varina, and daughter Winnie. It was here that he wrote *The Rise and Fall of the Confederate Government.*

After Davis's death, Beauvoir was used as a rest home for Confederate veterans, many of whom are buried in a cemetery on the grounds. Also in the cemetery is the Tomb of the Unknown Confederate Soldier.

Beauvoir, 2244 Beach Blvd., Biloxi, MS 39531, is open September through March, daily, 9:00–4:00; April through August, daily, 9:00–5:00. A museum contains mementos of Davis's public life and Confederate artifacts. Admission is $7.50 for adults, $6.75 for seniors, active military personnel, and AAA members, and $4.50 for students six to sixteen, free for children under six. For information phone 601-388-1313.

Brice's Cross Roads and Tupelo Battlefields

Baldwyn and Tupelo, Mississippi

They were minor battles, skirmishes really, remembered chiefly because they demonstrated the military genius of Nathan Bedford Forrest, the most feared of all Confederate cavalry leaders.

Forrest was born in poverty, educated himself, became a successful slave trader and plantation owner, joined the army as a private, rose to the rank of lieutenant general, and is best remembered for his philosophy of warfare: "War means fightin' and fightin' means killin'." He applied this belief with imagination and ferocity.

He became famous early in the war. He led his regiment through Grant's lines to escape from Fort Donelson. Time after time, he led successful raids behind enemy lines. But he was far more than a raider, which he clearly demonstrated at Brice's Cross Roads. There, in a head-on engagement, he inflicted one of the most humiliating defeats in the history of the U.S. Army.

In the spring of 1864, as General William T. Sherman drove his army south toward Atlanta, Forrest repeatedly struck at his supply line. Sherman sent General Samuel Sturgis with eight thousand troops into Mississippi to stop Forrest. Learning of this, Forrest concentrated his 3,500 troopers along the railroad near Brice's Cross Roads.

On the morning of June 10, 1864, Forrest surprised Sturgis, sending the Union force into a chaotic retreat toward Memphis. Forrest doggedly pursued the Union force for twenty-two miles. Sturgis lost 223 killed, 394 wounded, and 623 captured. Forrest captured sixteen of his eighteen guns, and the entire train of 250 vehicles, complete with 184 horses, rations, and ammunition.

The next month, Sherman gave orders "to make up a force and go out to follow Forrest to the death, if it costs $10,000 and breaks the Treasury." With fourteen thousand men, General A. J. Smith marched to Tupelo and built strong defensive works.

Forrest attacked Smith's position on July 14 but took heavy losses, and suffered a painful wound in the foot. Although holding the advantage, Smith, fearful that he was running out of supplies, lost his nerve and ordered a retreat.

After the war, Sherman summed up the accomplishments of the brilliant field commander: "I think Forrest was the most remarkable man our Civil War produced on either side."

Brice's Cross Roads Battlefield is six miles west of Baldwyn on MS 340, and twenty-five miles southwest of Tupelo. The park is small, but affords a view of much of the scene of action. There are no facilities at the park.

Tupelo National Battlefield has not been preserved but the engagement is commemorated at the one-acre park. Here the Confederates formed to attack the Union position. It is on Rte. 6, about a mile west of the intersection with U.S. 45. The park is unmanned, but at the **Tupelo Visitor Center,** a mile west of the battlefield, interpreters answer questions about the battle. (A more popular historic site in Tupelo is the house where Elvis Presley was born.) For information phone 601-680-4025 or 800-305-7417.

South of Tupelo, between West Point and Columbus on Hwy 50, is the **Waverley Plantation Mansion,** a National Historic Landmark Greek revival home. General Nathan Bedford Forrest was a friend and frequent visitor of the owner, Colonel George Hampton Young. During the war, Forrest spent three weeks recuperating here, living in the Egyptian Room and using it as his headquarters. Waverley has twenty acres of landscaped gardens with peacocks and black swans. Open daily; hours are seasonal. Admission is $7.50 for adults, children under six free. For information phone 601-494-1399.

The Mockingbird Inn

Tupelo, Mississippi

The Mockingbird Inn is a good place to make your headquarters in this interesting area. Innkeepers Jim and Sandy Gilmer named the inn after the state bird and decorated their guest rooms to suggest their favorite places—Mackinac Island, Paris, Athens, Venice, Africa, Florida, and Bavaria. The big house is comfortable and conveniently located, and breakfast is a joy.

The Tupelo battlefield is not preserved, but the one-acre **Tupelo National Battlefield** commemorates the engagement. (Rte. 6; 601-842-1572.) Also of interest is the **Tupelo Museum** (Rte. 6, 601-841-6438), which exhibits Civil War weapons and relics, archaeological finds, Indian artifacts, a log cabin, and other examples of indigenous architecture, including a one-room schoolhouse and a country store.

Address: 305 N. Gloster St., Tupelo, MS 38801;
  tel: 601-841-0286; fax: 601-840-4158.
Accommodations: Seven double rooms, all with private baths.
Amenities: Air-conditioning, off-street parking, phones and
  cable TV in rooms.
Rates: $$. Visa, MasterCard, and personal checks.
Restrictions: No children under ten, no smoking.

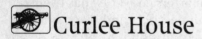Curlee House

Corinth, Mississippi

Generals favored this handsome 1857 Victorian house. At various times, Braxton Bragg, John Bell Hood, and Henry Halleck used it as their headquarters. Now restored, the house is a museum containing antebellum furniture, decorative objects, and Civil War memorabilia. The **Corinth Civil War Visitor Center** is located at the rear of the house.

Before the occupation of Corinth, General P. G. T. Beauregard stayed at the 1856 **Fish Pond House,** 708 Kilpatrick St., which now is a private home. General Albert S. Johnston, who was mortally wounded at Shiloh, made his headquarters at **Rose Cottage,** U.S. 45 at Fillmore St., and his body was brought here to lie in state after the battle. Rose Cottage also is a private home.

In the Battle of Corinth, General Beauregard, realizing how badly his Confederates were outnumbered, ordered a nighttime evacuation by railroad south toward Tupelo. To fool the Federals, when the empty trains rolled into town for the evacuation, the rebels cheered and bugles sounded as if reinforcements had arrived. The next morning the Federals found an empty town.

The Confederates attempted to recapture Corinth the following October, but were repulsed, with heavy casualties. **Battery Robinette,** on W. Linden St., was the site of the heaviest fighting.

The **Curlee House,** 705 Jackson St., is open daily; hours are seasonal. Admission is $2.50 for adults, $1.50 for children. For information phone 601-287-9501.

The General's Quarters

Corinth, Mississippi

The junction of two major railroads made this northeastern Mississippi town an important transit point for Confederate troops and supplies. In May 1862, more than 128,000 Federal troops surrounded the town, and the badly outnumbered Confederates left by train for Tupelo. That fall a Confederate attempt to retake the town was thrown back with heavy casualties.

This comfortable Victorian house wasn't built until 1870, but it is in the heart of the town's historic district, and Shiloh is just twenty-two miles to the north. Luke and Charlotte Doehner have decorated their inn tastefully with period antiques, and with advance notice will prepare dinner for guests. The self-guided Historic Corinth Walking Tour is a must. Pick up a map at the **Visitors Center** at the rear of the Curlee House, just down the street from the inn.

Address: 924 Fillmore St., Corinth, MS 38834;
tel: 601-286-3325; fax: 601-287-8188.

Accommodations: Five double rooms, all with private baths.

Amenities: Air-conditioning, on-premise parking, phones and
TV in guest rooms, laundry service, in-room computer
hookups, dinner and picnic lunches available (extra charge),
lawn tennis and croquet, concierge services.

Rates: $$, including full breakfast. Visa, Mastercard, Discover.

Restrictions: No children under ten, no pets, no smoking.

Millsaps Buie House

Jackson, Mississippi

This Queen Anne-style mansion was the home of Reuben
Webster Millsaps, a twice-wounded Confederate major,
banker, financier, and founder of Millsaps College. It was
designed by William Nichols, the architect of the Governor's
Mansion. It comes as a surprise to learn that when the house
was built in 1888, Jackson had a population of only 5,000, not
its current 400,000.

The house is furnished beautifully. In the parlor is a
French "courting bench" and pier mirrors capture images of
the grand piano. Guest rooms have period antiques, including
canopy beds, rosewood chairs, and marble-top tables. TVs are
concealed in old armoires. Business travelers often stop here,
and the phones in the rooms have computer dataports.

There's a lot of history nearby. Trenches and cannon may
be seen in Battlefield Park, at Langley St. and Terry Rd. In 1863,
after Sherman finished with Jackson, it was known as Chimney-
ville. City Hall, on S. President St., a field hospital during the
battle, was one of the few buildings to escape destruction in 1863.

Address: 628 N. State St., Jackson, MS 39202; tel. and fax: 601-
352-0221 and 800-784-0221.

Accommodations: Eleven double rooms, all with private baths.
Amenities: Air-conditioning, off-street parking, TV and radios.
Rates: Single, $$$. All major credit cards and personal checks.
Restrictions: No children under twelve, no pets, no smoking.

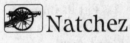

Natchez

Mississippi

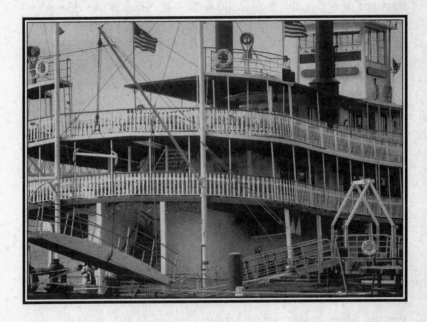

Steamboats carrying cotton to market in New Orleans made
Natchez rich, and planters from nearby plantations com-
peted to see who could build the most opulent mansion.

Natchez, like New Orleans, was occupied early in the war
and suffered little damage, and today the beauty and enchant-
ment of the Old South has been preserved. This town of twenty

thousand people has more outstanding examples of opulent Victorian architecture than any other place its size in the country.

Today Natchez seems beautiful and romantic—Greek revival mansions, manicured gardens and lawns, tree-shaded streets, and, of course, Southern hospitality. One of the oldest towns in the Mississippi Valley, Natchez has seen a lot of history. French, Spanish, English, Confederate, and U.S. flags have flown over Natchez, and each culture has left its imprint.

People come from all over the world for the **Natchez Pilgrimages,** one in late March and early April, and another in mid-October. They feature house tours and the **Confederate Pageant**. For details phone 800-647-6742. If your inn doesn't have a walking-tour map and the list of the antebellum houses that may be visited, pick them up at the **Natchez Visitors Bureau** at 422 Main St., or phone 800-647-6724 and they will be mailed to you.

To better understand wartime Natchez, visit **Longwood** at 140 Lower Woodville Rd. It is eloquent testimony to the devastating impact of the war on the cotton economy of the Deep South. The story of the hardships of the family who lived there "reared in the lap of luxury and reduced to poverty," has all the pathos of *Gone with the Wind* but with a twist: the family who lost everything was loyal to the Union. Open daily, 9:00–5:00. Admission is $5 for adults, $2.50 for children six to seventeen; free for children under six. For information phone 601-442-5193.

Windsor Ruins, a short detour from the Natchez Trace Pkwy., is a ghostly skeleton of twenty-three Corinthian columns. They once were part of a great mansion on the Mississippi River, built by slave labor between 1859 and 1861. During the war the roof was used by Confederates as an observation deck; later the house was a Federal field hospital. The ruins are on Rte. 552, ten miles west of Port Gibson. Open daily, dawn to dusk. Admission is free. For information phone 601-437-4551.

Monmouth
Natchez, Mississippi

The handsome mansion called Monmouth is a tribute to John A. Quitman, who once was considered the most popular man in the country. He was a hero-general of the Mexican War, then governor of Mississippi, and later a congressman.

In 1826, Quitman purchased Monmouth for his bride. Their chamber, now a guest room, has a massive four-poster tester bed, Oriental carpeting, and a fireplace. He died in this room in 1858, after an illness caused, reportedly, by being poisoned while attending a banquet for President Buchanan.

Monmouth is a mini-museum. On display is a sword presented to Quitman by President Polk in honor of his bravery and leadership in battle, and other mementos of a distinguished career.

There are seven rooms in the main house, four in the slave quarters, and seventeen more in buildings throughout the garden area. All are handsomely appointed with canopied beds and armoires. Breakfast is served in the Marguerite Guercio reception room, as well as in the garden area.

Monmouth manages to be charming and historically fascinating at the same time, no mean feat even in Natchez, where charm and history are waiting around every corner.

Address: 36 Melrose Ave., Natchez, MS 39120; tel: 601-442-5852 or 800-828-4531; fax: 601-446-7762.

Accommodations: Twenty-eight rooms including ten suites, all with private baths.

Amenities: Air-conditioning, off-street parking, phones and TV in rooms, dinner available in the mansion nightly, fishing pond on 26-acre grounds.

Rates: $$$. All major credit cards and personal checks.

Restrictions: No children under fourteen, no pets, restricted smoking.

Dunleith

Natchez, Mississippi

This is everyone's dream of a Southern plantation house—a massive white raised cottage with Greek revival details surrounded by twenty-eight columns, restored to perfection and now a National Historic Monument. It stands on forty landscaped acres with stables and other outbuildings.

Dunleith was built in 1856, when cotton was king. The house is almost a museum: French Zuber wallpaper in the dining room, V'Soske carpet in the front parlor, and a Louis XV ormolu-mounted Linke table in the front parlor. Guests are greeted with lemonade, and baskets of snacks are in their beautifully furnished rooms. A plantation breakfast is served in the old poultry house, which now has exposed beams and big windows. At night Dunleith's grounds are lighted to duplicate the romance of moonlight.

Address: 84 Homochitto St., Natchez, MS 39120;
  tel: 601-446-8500 or 800-433-2445.
Accommodations: Eleven guest rooms, eight in the courtyard
  wing, three in the main house, all with private baths.
Amenities: Air-conditioning, parking on grounds, TV in
  rooms, house tour.
Rates: $$–$$$. Visa, MasterCard, and Discover.
Restrictions: No children under eighteen, no pets, restricted smoking.

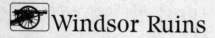Windsor Ruins

Port Gibson, Mississippi

Twenty-three towering Corinthian columns evoke powerful feelings for the South that was consumed by the Civil War. They stand here, near the extinct town of Bruinsburg, itself a victim of the war.

The Windsor mansion, built by slave labor between 1859 and 1861, was near the place where Grant's army crossed the river to march on Jackson, Mississippi. Both sides found Windsor useful: Confederates used its high roof as an observation platform; Federal soldiers later used the house as a field hospital.

The house survived the war, but the columns were the only survivors of a fire in 1890. In *Life on the Mississippi*, Mark Twain recalled that when he piloted a Mississippi River steamboat, he used Windsor as a landmark.

The **Windsor Ruins,** on Rte. 552, ten miles west of Port Gibson, are open daily, dawn to dusk. The ruins are unattended. Admission is free. For information phone 601-437-4351.

Oak Square Plantation
Port Gibson, Mississippi

On his way to Vicksburg in 1863, Grant marched his 25,000 troops through this small town, remarking that it was "too beautiful to burn." Oak Square, built around 1850, was one of the reasons the town was so beautiful.

Oak Square is now an inn owned and operated by Mr. and Mrs. William D. Lum, who enjoy regaling guests with tales of the war. Mr. Lum's great-grandfather, a Confederate officer, was killed in the war in 1864 and his servant, who traveled with him, walked 250 miles to tell the family of his master's death.

Two Union generals stayed at Mr. Lum's ancestral home nearby, and thirty years later two pieces of family silver were returned by a Yankee soldier who camped there.

At the Mississippi, seven miles to the west, is the **Grand Gulf Military Monument,** the site of the opening shots of the Battle of Port Gibson.

Oak Square, with thirty rooms, is the town's largest and most palatial mansion. It has been restored and furnished with family heirlooms and contains a collection of Civil War memorabilia. The manicured grounds have a courtyard, fountain, gazebo, and, of course, massive oaks. Oak Square has been awarded four diamonds by the AAA.

Address: 1207 Church St., Port Gibson, MS 39150;
   tel: 601-437-4350 or 800-729-0240; fax: 601-437-5768.
Accommodations: Twelve guests rooms, all with private baths.
Amenities: Air-conditioning, off-street parking, house and grounds tour, canopied beds, arrangements made for motorcoach tours of the area.
Rates: $$–$$$. All major credit cards and personal checks.
Restrictions: Children by prior approval, no pets, no smoking.

Vicksburg Battlefield

Vicksburg, Mississippi

I f the Union could control the Mississippi River, then Texas, Arkansas, and Louisiana would be cut off from the rest of the Confederacy. But to control the Mississippi, Vicksburg would have to be captured, and Vicksburg, situated on a bluff two hundred feet above the river, was known as the "Gibraltar of the Confederacy."

For months, General Ulysses S. Grant attempted to get at Vicksburg from the opposite side of the river. His army chopped through forests and swamps and dug canals. All attempts to cross the river failed.

Grant audaciously marched his 44,000 troops down the western bank of the Mississippi. An attempt to cross the river was repulsed, but the Union troops were able to cross at Bruinsburg on April 30, 1863. Then the army marched fif-

teen miles northeast and took Jackson, the state capital, on
July 21, 1863.

Then Grant proceeded to defeat General John C. Pemberton's forces at Champion Hill and Big Black River Bridge.
Coordinating his attack with the gunboats of Admiral David
Porter, which were able to fire on the city from the river, his
army surrounded the city.

During the siege many of the townspeople moved into
caves in the nearby hills. The siege lasted forty-seven days,
from May 22 to July 4. When Pemberton surrendered to
Grant, President Lincoln said gratefully, "The Father of Waters
again goes unvexed to the sea."

Vicksburg National Military Park borders the eastern and
northern sections of the city. The entrance and **Visitor Center**
are on Clay Street (U.S. 80), exit 4B off of I-20. Audiovisual
aids and exhibits at the center portray the history of the campaign. A sixteen-mile self-guided driving tour begins at the
center. There are monuments all along the way, but the only
surviving structure in the park is the Shirley House, which
Union troops called the "white house." During the siege, it was
the headquarters of the 45th Illinois Infantry. The park is
open daily, 8:00–5:00, except Christmas. Admission is $4 per
car. For information phone 601-636-0583.

Just off the tour road is the **USS *Cairo* Museum,** featuring
a gunboat that was sunk by a mine during the siege, and later
retrieved from the river and restored. An audiovisual program
tells of the sinking and the role of gunboats in the war. Open
daily, hours seasonal, except Christmas. Admission is free. For
information phone 601-636-2199.

In the city, the **Old Court House Museum,** Court Square,
1008 Cherry St., was where Grant raised the U.S. flag on July 4,
1863, signifying the end of the siege. In the Confederate
Room are weapons and documents of the siege. Open daily,
hours seasonal, except on major holidays. For information
phone 601-636-0741.

The Vanishing Glory is a thirty-minute wide-screen audiovisual presentation dramatizing the siege of the city, based on

the diaries and other writings of people who lived through it. It is shown daily on the hour at the Strand Theatre, 717 Clay St. Admission is $5 for adults, $3 for students, free for children under three; group rates and special showtimes available upon request. For information call 601-634-1863.

To see all the sites associated with Grant's brilliant campaign and the siege of Vicksburg, take two or three days and follow **The Vicksburg Campaign Trail**. The stops include Big Black Battlefield, Champion Hill Battlefield, the Battlefield and Confederate Cemetery in Raymond, the Grand Gulf Military Monument Park, the Jackson Battlefield, the Vicksburg National Military Park, and the Windsor Ruins. "A Guide to the Campaign & Siege of Vicksburg" describes a self-guided tour of these sites and is available free from the Mississippi Division of Tourism Development, PO Box 1705, Ocean Springs, MS 39566, or by phoning 800-WARMEST.

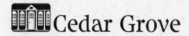 Cedar Grove

Vicksburg, Mississippi

When Admiral Farragut's squadron steamed up the Mississippi River and fired on Vicksburg, several cannonballs struck this Greek revival mansion. One smashed the front door and another lodged in the door casing between the twin parlors, where it remains.

After the city surrendered, General Grant stayed in this house for three days. The bed he slept in is still in use in the General Grant Suite. This mansion was built from 1840 to 1858, and many of the original furnishings remain, including several monumental gold-leaf pier mirrors, the silver, and tableware.

Hoop-skirted ladies conduct tours of the house, telling fascinating stories of the people who lived here during the war. The inn has a restaurant in the main house, which is open for dinner every evening except Monday. It is also the setting for the leisurely plantation breakfast.

Address: 2200 Oak St., Vicksburg, MS 19180; tel: 601-636-1605; fax: 601-634-6126.
Accommodations: Thirteen double rooms and twelve suites, all with private baths.
Amenities: Air-conditioning, off-street parking, phone and TV in all rooms, swimming pool, hot tub, tennis court, and croquet.
Rates: $$–$$$, including house tour and full Southern breakfast. American Express, Visa, MasterCard, Discover, and personal checks.
Restrictions: No pets, restricted smoking.

Rosswood

Lorman, Mississippi

On July 4 and 5, 1864, a regimental-sized battle was fought near here, called the Battle of Coleman's Plantation by the North and the Battle of the Cotton Bales by the South. This mansion was shelled, the kitchen building was hit and destroyed, and the wounded from both sides were brought in and cared for by Marybella Wade, the mistress of the house.

According to a local legend, the ghost of a Union officer who died in the battle appears from time to time in Rosswood, greeting guests with a cheery "Hello!"

The 1857 Greek revival house is a Mississippi landmark and listed in the National Register of Historic Places. The rooms are spacious, with fifteen-foot ceilings and heart-of-pine floors, and are beautifully decorated with antiques. The architect, David Shroder, also designed Windsor, the ruins of which are nearby (see pages 196–197).

After the war, Rosswood was the residence for a number
of years of Mrs. Elizabeth Hamer, the favorite niece of Jefferson Davis. Innkeepers Walt and Jean Hylander point out
that Rosswood still is a plantation, although the cash crop now
is not cotton, but Christmas trees.

Address: Hwy. 552 East, Lorman, MS 39096; tel: 601-437-4215
  or 800-533-5889; fax: 601-437-6888; E-mail:
  hylander@aol.com. Rosswood is midway between Natchez
  and Vicksburg, just east of U.S. 61. From the Natchez Trace
  take the Rte. 552 exit.
Accommodations: Four double rooms, all with private baths.
Amenities: Air-conditioning, off-street parking, ceiling fans,
  phones, color TV with VCR in rooms, house tour, swimming
  pool and whirlpool spa.
Rates: $$$. All credit cards and personal checks.
Restrictions: No pets, restricted smoking.

Rosemont Plantation
Woodville, Mississippi

This working plantation was the boyhood home of Jefferson
Davis, the first and only president of the Confederacy. The
handsome planter's cottage was built in 1810 by his father,
Samuel Davis, who brought his wife and ten children here
from Kentucky, where Jefferson, the youngest child, was born.

After attending nearby Jefferson College, Jefferson Davis
entered West Point in 1824. In 1835 he married Sarah Taylor,
resigned from the army, and became a planter near Vicksburg.
A few months later, Sarah died of malaria and Davis would
spend a decade as a near recluse, mourning her death.

In 1845 Davis married Varina Howell, who was from
Natchez. He became a U.S. congressman in 1845. He resigned
to lead Mississippi troops in the Mexican War, emerged a

hero, and was appointed to the U.S. Senate. He served as secretary of war under President Franklin Pierce. After having returned to the Senate, he resigned his seat when Mississippi seceded and was elected president of the Confederacy.

Five generations of Davises lived at Rosemont until it was sold in 1895. Many furnishings are either original to the house or belonged to various members of the Davis family. Near the house is the rose garden planted by Jane Davis, for which the plantation was named. Beyond the cottage are split-rail fences, outbuildings typical of a nineteenth-century working plantation, and the Davis family cemetery. Jefferson Davis, however, is buried at Hollywood Cemetery in Richmond, Virginia.

A cabin near the house has been made into comfortable guest quarters. Afternoon drinks are served on the gallery, and guests are given a tour of the house and the plantation. Several nature trails wind through the property.

Address: Hwy. 24 East, PO Box 814, Woodville, MS 39669; tel: 601-888-6809; fax: 601-888-3606.

Accommodations: A cottage with living room, bedroom, kitchen, and bath.

Amenities: Afternoon drinks on the gallery, house tour, nature trails.

Rates: $$–$$$. Visa, MasterCard.

Restrictions: No pets.

LOUISIANA

Lloyd Hall

Nottoway Plantation

Nicolas M. Benachi House

Le Richelieu

Lloyd Hall

Cheneyville, Louisiana

One of the owners of the insurance company Lloyds of London once had a ne'er-do-well son, William, to whom they gave a handsome sum of money, on the provision that he change the spelling of his famous surname and emigrate to America, never to return. He wound up here, where in the 1820s he built this Federal Georgian manor.

Union troops, who burned most of the town in 1864, believed Lloyd had lied to them and hanged him near the house. His English relatives, who undoubtedly predicted he would end badly, were not disappointed.

In 1948, the Fitzgeralds bought the 640-acre property for grazing land, only to discover the old manor, covered with brambles and undergrowth. Now restored, it is a showplace, completely furnished with period antiques.

The Fitzgeralds live in the manor, and guests stay in the renovated outbuildings. Beulah Davis takes guests through the house and tells them of the ghost of William Lloyd, who still oversees the property, and Harry, a young Union soldier who died on the third floor. Harry, it seems, plays the violin on moonlit nights.

Address: 298 Lloyd Bridge Rd., Cheneyville, LA 71325; tel: 318-776-5641 or 800-240-8135; fax: 318-776-5886.

Accommodations: Four guest rooms, all with private baths.

Amenities: Air-conditioning, off-street parking, swimming pool, mountain bikes; all rooms have wood-burning fireplaces. Wine or soft drinks on arrival.

Rates: $$–$$$, including continental breakfast. All major credit cards and personal checks.

Restrictions: No pets, restricted smoking.

Nottoway Plantation

White Castle, Louisiana

Nottoway is the largest antebellum plantation mansion in the South, and an outstanding example of the opulent lifestyle enjoyed by the planter aristocracy before the war. It has three stories, sixty-six rooms, and encloses 53,000 square feet.

The owner, John Randolph, a planter from Nottoway County, Virginia, had seven thousand acres of sugar cane, and some seven hundred field slaves and fifty-seven house slaves. In 1862, as Union troops moved up the Mississippi, Randolph took his slaves and went to Texas to raise cotton.

Mrs. Randolph remained at Nottoway. When a Union gunboat began firing on the house, she went out on the balcony to face down the Yankees. By chance, the boat's captain had been a guest at Nottoway before the war, recognized Mrs. Randolph, and ordered the firing stopped. Federal troops later encamped on the grounds, but never bothered the house.

Today there are guest rooms in the main mansion and the overseer's cottage, which overlooks sculpted gardens and a duck pond. All have four-poster beds, armoires, and fresh flowers. At Nottoway you magically become Rhett or Scarlett. A restaurant on the premises serves lunch and dinner. For an extra charge, guests can dine in the mansion's dining room.

Address: LA Hwy. 1 (PO Box 160), White Castle, LA 70788; tel: 504-545-2730; fax 504-545-8632.

Accommodations: Ten rooms, all with private baths, and three suites.

Amenities: Air-conditioning, parking, restaurant, pool, gift shop, free house tour.

Rates: $$$, including continental wake-up breakfast and full breakfast. All major credit cards accepted.

Restrictions: No pets, restricted smoking.

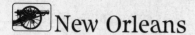# New Orleans

Louisiana

In 1860, with the largest cotton market in the world, New Orleans was the wealthiest city, per capita, in the United States. The decision to secede was unpopular with many in the city, particularly merchants, whose livelihood depended on trade with the North.

The Union began blockading the Mississippi on May 26, 1861, cutting the city off from the imports it had come to rely on. By the next spring, Union ships began bombarding the forts below the city. Troop ships passed the forts and headed upriver to New Orleans. Warehouses were burned and looters swarmed throughout the city.

New Orleans was occupied on May 1, 1862, by General Benjamin Butler, who soon alienated the populace. He was nicknamed "Spoons" because he allegedly stole silver from his hosts. Ladies hired artists to paint a likeness of the general on the inside of their chamber pots. He ordered that the words "The Union Must and Shall Be Preserved" be carved on the base of the statue of Andrew Jackson in Jackson Square.

What most angered Southerners, though, was his Order No. 28, which stated, ". . . any female who shall, by word, gesture, or movement, insult or show contempt for any officer or soldier of the United States, she shall be regarded and held liable to be treated as a woman of the town plying her avocation." This order contributed to Butler's removal from New Orleans on December 16, 1862. The city would remain occupied by Federal troops through the war's end.

Several Crescent City sites have Civil War interest. The **Confederate Museum,** Camp and Howard Sts., the oldest museum in the state, displays flags, uniforms, weapons, medical instruments, currency, and personal effects of Jefferson Davis, Robert E. Lee, and other Confederate leaders. Open daily except Sunday, 10:00–4:00. Admission is $5 for adults, $4 for seniors and students, and $2 for children. For information phone 504-523-4522.

The **Old U.S. Mint,** 400 Esplanade Ave. For a short time during the war, this was the only mint in the Confederacy. Operated from 1838 to 1909, it is now part of the **Louisiana State Museum**. The building has been restored and contains many popular exhibits and a collection of historic documents. Open Tuesday–Sunday, 9:00–5:00. Admission is $4 for adults, $3 for seniors, teens, and active military personnel, and free for children under twelve. For information phone 504-568-6968.

In **Jackson Square** the equestrian statue of Andrew Jackson was the world's first equestrian statue with more than one hoof unsupported. The sculptor, the American Clark Mills, had never seen an equestrian statue, and hadn't known the pose was thought impossible.

On U.S. 90, twenty-three miles east of downtown New Orleans, is the **Fort Pike State Commemorative Area**. The Louisiana militia captured Fort Pike before the actual start of the war and held it until Union forces took the city in 1862. In spite of much activity, not a single cannon was ever fired in battle from the fort. Open daily, 9:00–5:00. Admission is $2 for adults; seniors and children under twelve free. Museum and picnic area. For information phone 504-662-5703.

Terrell House

New Orleans, Louisiana

When you arrive at this handsome Greek revival house in the lower Garden District, a surprise is waiting for you inside—one of the city's most impressive collections of antiques. The house, built in 1858 by a cotton merchant, is currently owned by the Hogan family, whose collections of gaslight fixtures and lamps, Louisiana and European furniture, Oriental rugs, and antique carnival memorabilia are on display throughout the house. In one of the twin parlors a glass case contains miniature carved antique furnishings, and in the hallway is a full set of 1850 salesmen's sample furniture. The dining room, where breakfast and afternoon cocktails are served, has a magnificent Waterford crystal chandelier.

Guest rooms in the main house have balconies overlooking a beautifully landscaped courtyard with a fountain and a crape myrtle tree. Some of the rooms contain beds or armoires carved by the master New Orleans furniture maker Prudent Mallard. Four guest rooms are in the carriage house that opens onto the courtyard. Bobby Hogan operates Terrell House in a warm, comfortable manner. His wife, Cindy, who occasionally cooks dinner for guests, is known for her flair with regional dishes such as crawfish étouffée.

Address: 1441 Magazine St., New Orleans, LA 70130; tel and fax: 504-524-9859 or 800-878-9859.

Accommodations: Eight double guest rooms with baths, two suites.

Amenities: All guest rooms have air-conditioning, phones, and cable TV; off-street parking, afternoon cocktails, Jacuzzi in courtyard.

Rates: $$–$$$. All major credit cards accepted.

Restrictions: Call in advance regarding children, no pets, restricted smoking.

Nicolas M. Benachi House
New Orleans, Louisiana

This exquisite Greek revival house near the French Quarter was constructed on Bayou Road in 1858 for Nicolas M. Benachi, cotton broker and consul of Greece. It cost $18,000 at a time when beef was five cents a pound. Bayou Road was the old New Orleans Trace, a trail on the Esplanade Ridge that connected the river with the bayous and their environs. Benachi called his house the *Rendezvous des Chasseurs* (meeting place of the hunters), and from here he and his friends would hunt the nearby swamps.

Today, the house retains its original details: fourteen-foot ceilings with banded cornices and medallions, carved black marble mantels, rococo revival chandeliers, Greek key doorways, and heart-of-pine floors. Many of the period furnishings were made by the New Orleans master cabinetmakers, Mallard, Seignouret, and Barjon. Each of the four guest rooms is named for a Benachi son or daughter.

The gardens, with pink Belgian flagstones, set the house off to perfection. It's not surprising to learn that two recent movies featured the house. Hosts Jim Derbes and Cecilia Rau give guests a tour of the award-winning restoration.

Address: 2257 Bayou Rd., New Orleans, LA 70119; tel: 504-525-7040 or 800-308-7040; fax: 504-525-9760; E-mail: cottonenolabb.com. Internet browsers can visit their website at www.nolabb.com.

Accommodations: Four guest rooms, two with private baths, two with a shared bath.

Amenities: Air-conditioning, off-street parking, TV sets available on request, library, bathrobes provided, walking distance to French Quarter; a friendly Labrador dog is in residence.

Rates: $$–$$$, including full breakfast and evening beverage. Major credit cards and personal checks.

Restrictions: No children, no pets, no smoking.

Beauregard-Keyes House

New Orleans, Louisiana

The fiery Confederate general, Pierre Gustave Toutant Beauregard, known as "The Little Napoleon," lived in this 1826 Greek revival house for two years after the war. A native of New Orleans, Beauregard achieved fame by commanding the troops who fired on Fort Sumter in Charleston Harbor in 1861 and as the victorious general at Manassas, Virginia, the first major land battle of the war. However, he angered Jefferson Davis and was sent to serve in the West. He took over the Confederate army at Shiloh after the death of Albert Sidney Johnston, but was driven from the field by Grant.

In the 1940s, the house was the home of Frances Parkinson Keyes, who set several of her best-selling novels in New Orleans. The house contains some furnishings of Beauregard and Keyes.

The **Beauregard-Keyes House,** 1113 Chartres St., New Orleans, LA 70116, is open daily, 10:00–3:00, except Sunday and major holidays. Civil War artifacts have been unearthed nearby. Docents conduct guided tours of the house and servants' quarters from 10:00–3:00, when the last tour starts. Admission is $4 for adults, $3 for seniors, and $1.50 for children twelve and under. For information phone 504-523-7257.

Le Richelieu

New Orleans, Louisiana

This inn was created from two adjacent French Quarter buildings: an 1850 Greek revival house (one of five in a row built by a father for his children) and a 1902 four-story macaroni factory, and the result is a curious but pleasing mélange. It was named for Cardinal Richelieu (whose portrait hangs in the lobby across from the front desk), the powerful prime minister of Louis XIII, the king who once owned the land where the inn now stands.

Many discerning travelers consider Le Richelieu their secret hideaway in the Crescent City. Overlooking the courtyard is a bar and restaurant, which serves light continental fare. Both are frequented by New Orleanians who live nearby.

Le Richelieu offers guests two important amenities: off-street parking, a rare commodity in the Quarter, and peace and quiet, another rare commodity here, yet the Quarter's many attractions are but a short walk away.

Address: 1234 Chartres St., New Orleans, LA 70116;
tel: 504-529-2492 or 800-535-9653; fax: 504-524-8179.
Accommodations: Eighty-six rooms, including seventeen suites.
Amenities: Air-conditioning, ceiling fans, free off-street parking, satellite TV and refrigerators in rooms, swimming pool, concierge, valet service, bellhops, room service, balconies.
Rates: $$–$$$. All major credit cards.
Restrictions: No pets.

Mississippi Queen

S teamboats were commandeered by the military during the war to transport troops and supplies along the Mississippi and its tributaries. They played an important role in Grant's capture of Fort Donelson and Nathaniel Banks's Red River Campaign. Today passengers can travel those same routes aboard two authentic steam-powered paddle wheelers and visit and see Civil War sites accompanied by experts on the war.

Civil War Steamboatin' Vacations are seven-day cruises in May and June on the *Mississippi Queen* and in September on the *Delta Queen*, herself a National Historic Landmark. Among

the experts who give lectures aboard and guided tours ashore are Richard McMurry, author of *Two Great Rebel Armies*, William C. "Jack" Davis, consultant to the A&E Network's *Civil War Journal*, and James I. Robertson Jr., author of *The Stonewall Brigade*. (Mr. Robertson, a deacon of the Anglican Catholic Church, conducts a special Civil War Sunday service using hymns and texts from the period.) In addition, actor James Getty presents his portrayal of Abraham Lincoln, and balladeer Bobby Horton performs the songs of the Blue and Gray. The cruises travel between Memphis and Chattanooga, and Nashville and Memphis. Each cruise makes several shore visits to historic sites.

Civil War Vacation Cruises are offered by The Delta Queen Steamboat Co. Fares for the week-long cruises begin at $990 per person, based on double occupancy, and include all meals, activities, and entertainment. For information phone a travel agent.

ARKANSAS

Crescent Cottage Inn

The Empress of Little Rock

Crescent Cottage Inn
Eureka Springs, Arkansas

In the Victorian era, well-to-do families needed a proper reason to take a summer holiday. The spiritual uplift of a Chatauqua meeting, perhaps, or the physical well-being induced by drinking water from mineral springs. This gingerbread town came into being practically overnight as families flocked to enjoy its mineral waters and clear mountain air.

One promoter of Eureka Springs was Powell Clayton, a Union general and the first postwar governor of Arkansas, who built the Crescent Cottage Inn in 1881. Today the mansion has been restored to its original elegance and furnished with antiques.

Innkeepers Ralph and Phyllis Becker pamper their guests with early coffee, a delicious full breakfast, and afternoon tea or wine. Crescent Cottage Inn is a superb inn, one of the best in the country. It is a short walk from the good restaurants and shops in the historic downtown area and an easy drive to the battlefield at Pea Ridge.

Address: 211 Spring St., Eureka Springs, AR 72632; tel: 501-253-6022; fax: 501-253-6234; E-mail: raphael@ipa.net.
Accommodations: Four double rooms, all with private baths.
Amenities: Air-conditioning, parking, rooms have Jacuzzis; some have fireplaces and refrigerators; all have phones, TVs, and VCRs. Complimentary soft drinks.
Rates: $$–$$$. Visa, MasterCard, Discover, and personal checks.
Restrictions: No children under twelve, no pets, restricted smoking.

🎖️Pea Ridge Battlefield

Pea Ridge, Arkansas

On March 7 and 8, 1862, a battle fought here, near the Elkhorn Tavern, kept Missouri in the Union. It was one of the most important battles of the war fought west of the Mississippi River.

Confederate general Earl Van Dorn planned to march from Arkansas into southern Missouri and retake St. Louis. When his seventeen-thousand-man army approached a strongly entrenched Federal force of eleven thousand under General Samuel Curtis south of Pea Ridge, Van Dorn abandoned his supply train and slipped behind him.

Federal scouts (among them, Wild Bill Hickok) observed the maneuver. Alerted, Curtis turned his back on his fortifications and prepared to meet Van Dorn's two-pronged attack.

On the first day of the battle, the Federals held their ground on their left flank southeast of Pea Ridge, and gave ground slowly in bitter fighting on their right around Elkhorn Tavern.

The next day, exhausted and low on ammunition, the rebels broke and ran under Curtis's determined counterattack, led by German immigrants under General Franz Sigel.

Pea Ridge was the only major battle in which Indian troops participated as regular troops. (The Confederates recruited about one thousand Cherokees from the Indian territory, now Oklahoma.) The Indians, having never before seen field cannon, were so awed by the power of the artillery that they eventually took to the woods.

Pea Ridge National Military Park is thirty miles northeast of Fayetteville, and an easy drive from Eureka Springs. The **Visitor Center** has a collection of arms, uniforms, artifacts and historical photographs. A slide presentation describes the battle and its significance. A self-guided auto tour goes along a seven-mile loop of the battlefield. The park is open daily, 8:00–5:00, except Thanksgiving, Christmas, and New Year's

Day. The battle is reenacted in the spring, and living history demonstrations are given in the summer and early fall. Admission is $2 for adults, children under sixteen free, $4 for cars. For information phone 501-451-8122.

Two other sites of interest are in the area. **Headquarters House,** 118 E. Dickson St., Fayetteville, was used at various times for both the Federal and Confederate armies. The Battle of Fayetteville was fought on the house grounds and across the street on April 18, 1863. The battle is reenacted here on the third Saturday in August. Open Monday, 10:00–12:00, Thursday, 1:00–4:00, and Saturday, 10:00–12:00. Tours by appointment. Admission is free. For information phone 501-521-2970.

Ten miles west of Fayetteville on U.S. 62 is the **Prairie Grove Battlefield State Park**. On December 7, 1862, the last major battle fought in northwest Arkansas took place here and it paved the way for control of the region by the Union army. The battle is reenacted the first weekend in December in even-numbered years. Open daily, 8:00–nightfall (museum open 8:00–5:00). Admission is $2.50 for adults, $1.50 for children. For information phone 501-846-2990.

The Old State House
Little Rock, Arkansas

One of the most beautiful buildings in the state, the Old State House is also one of the most historically significant. Opened in 1836, the year Arkansas was admitted to the Union, the legislature met here until the present capitol was built in 1911.

The 1861 secession convention was held here, and in 1863 the Confederate state government fled the area and the town was occupied by Union troops. General Frederick Steele quartered his army in the Old State House during the occupation.

The **Old State House Museum,** 300 W. Markham St., is a museum with six rooms furnished to show how tastes in the state changed over the years. Five galleries have changing history and art exhibits. On the lawn is "Lady Baxter," a cannon that dates from the Civil War. It is open Monday–Saturday, 9:00–5:00, and Sunday, 1:00–5:00. Admission is free. For information phone 501-324-9685.

The Empress of Little Rock

Little Rock, Arkansas

James Hornibrook, a prosperous saloon keeper, determined to give his family the finest house in the city, built this magnificent Queen Anne-style mansion in 1888. Among its many features: a divided stairway, stained glass, a three-and-a-half-story corner tower, and 7,500 square feet of interior space. Mr. Hornibrook, however, died shortly after the house was completed.

Over the years the mansion has been a women's college and a nursing home, and was finally divided up into apartments. Bob Blair and Sharon Welch-Blair bought the dilapidated eyesore, gave it the restoration it deserved, and turned it into a charming inn.

A Victorian atmosphere pervades the house. Bric-a-brac is everywhere. Floral Aubusson rugs cover the parquet floors, complemented by large-patterned wallpaper. The house, in the city's Quapaw Quarter Historic District, is on the National Register. The *National Geographic Traveler* described the Empress of Little Rock as "one of the loveliest buildings in the state." It is the only inn in Arkansas with a four-diamond rating from AAA.

Address: 2120 S. Louisiana St., Little Rock, AR 72206; tel: 501-374-7966.

Accommodations: Five guest rooms, all with private baths.

Amenities: Climate-controlled rooms, air-conditioning, off-street parking, rooms have clock-radios and phones, TV in room on request, exercise trail nearby, laundry service available, fax and copier available, computer dataports available.

Rates: $$–$$$, including choice of early-bird continental breakfast or gourmet brunch.

Restrictions: No children under ten, no pets, no smoking.

MISSOURI

*The Historic Mansion
at Elfindale*

Lafayette House

Walnut Street Inn

Garth Woodside Mansion

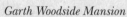

Ulysses S. Grant National Historic Site

St. Louis, Missouri

After Grant resigned from the army in 1854, he and his wife, Julia, lived on a tract of land near St. Louis that had been a wedding present from Julia's father.

Grant farmed, sold cordwood, and tried his hand at selling real estate in the city. He was successful at none of these endeavors, and in 1860 the family moved to Galena, Illinois, where Grant's father owned a tannery.

While in Missouri, Grant built this large Southern-style log home. It was roomy but ugly. Julia wrote to a friend: "The little house looked so unattractive that we facetiously decided to call it 'Hardscrabble.' " The house, which stands now on five of its original one thousand acres, gives a glimpse of the Grants at what was probably the lowest point of their lives.

The **Ulysses S. Grant National Historic Site** is open daily, 9:00–5:00, except Thanksgiving, Christmas, and New Year's Day. Rangers give building tours. Admission is free. The site is immediately across from the Anheuser-Busch "Grant's Farm" attraction. From I-270, exit at Gravois Rd. and go northeast about 2.5 miles. The site is a half-mile down on the left at 7400 Grant Road. For information phone 314-842-3298.

The Historic Mansion at Elfindale

Springfield, Missouri

Springfield was a military objective in the war. The Confederates occupied the town in the Battle of Wilson's Creek in 1861, but Union forces recaptured it the next year. Later, numerous attempts to retake Springfield failed. Wild Bill Hickok was stationed here as a scout and spy for Federal forces.

This handsome Queen Anne-style inn was built as a private home in 1892, and was sold to an order of nuns in 1906; it was a Catholic girls' school until 1964. It now is owned by a local church and managed as an inn by Jeff Wells.

The mansion is big. It contains 22,000 square feet with thirty-five rooms, of which thirteen are guest suites. The rooms on the main floor are used occasionally for weddings and receptions.

Address: 1701 S. Fort, Springfield, MO 65807;
 tel: 417-831-5400 or 800-443-0237; fax: 417-831-2965.
Accommodations: Thirteen guest rooms, all with private baths.
Amenities: Air-conditioning, off-street parking, room phones.
Rates: $$–$$$. All major credit cards and personal checks.

Restrictions: No children under ten, no pets, no smoking, no alcoholic beverages allowed on premises.

Lafayette House

St. Louis, Missouri

James B. Eads, a self-taught river engineer, built this house in 1876 as a wedding present for his daughter. When the war shut down river traffic, St. Louis commerce was paralyzed. Eads proposed building seven ironclad gunboats to help the Union forces. In a mere sixty-three days, he built the ironclads that Grant used to clear the Mississippi and cut the Confederacy in two. After the war, in 1874, he constructed the first bridge to span the Mississippi River, which was also the world's first arched steel truss bridge.

Hosts Nancy Buhr and Annalise Millet have furnished the three-story Queen Anne with a pleasing mixture of antiques and contemporary furniture, and the house was recently rated a two-diamond inn by AAA.

Address: 2156 Lafayette Ave., St. Louis, MO 63104; tel: 314-772-4429 or 800-641-8965; fax: 314-664-2156.
Accommodations: Six double rooms, three with private baths.
Amenities: Air-conditioning, phones in rooms, TV, VCR, and video library.
Rates: $$. All major credit cards and personal checks.
Restrictions: Limited facility for children, call first; no pets, no smoking.

🔫 Wilson's Creek Battlefield

Republic, Missouri

Missouri seemed to be on its way out of the Union when the Battle of Wilson's Creek was fought here on August 10, 1861. The governor, pro-Confederate Claiborne Jackson, had called out the state militia but failed in his attempt to seize the U.S. arsenal in St. Louis.

Governor Jackson, General Sterling Price, and their 5,170 troops retreated to the southwestern part of the state, where they were joined by five thousand Confederate troops commanded by General Ben McCulloch.

In pursuit was Brigadier General Nathaniel Lyon, and some 5,400 Union soldiers. On August 2, they overwhelmed a vanguard of Confederates near Springfield. During the fighting, however, Lyon learned that he was badly outnumbered.

Determined to press on, Lyon launched a surprise attack at dawn on August 10. The Confederates, encamped near Wilson's Creek, reacted quickly. Union forces supporting Lyon were driven back. Colonel Franz Sigel led his German-Americans into a flanking attack, taking the rebels by surprise. His attack faltered when he mistook some Confederates for Union troops. They tore into Sigel's troops, scattering them. This enabled the Confederates to concentrate on Lyon's forces on the crest of a ridge.

Lyon was slain and by late morning the Union troops were retreating toward Springfield. The Union lost 1,317 men, the Confederates, 1,222. Price would win another battle at Lexington, but the Confederates were never able to get Missouri out of the Union. During the rest of the war, Missouri would have two state governments, one Union and one Confederate.

Wilson's Creek National Battlefield is three miles east of Republic and ten miles southwest of Springfield, Missouri. The **Visitor Center** has a film, map, and museum that inform visitors about the battle and its relevance to the war. The park is open daily 8:00–5:00, except Christmas and New Year's Day. Admission is $2 for adults, $4 for a family. During summer months, tours and living-history demonstrations are held at Bloody Hill and the Ray House, which served as a field hospital during the battle. A self-guided driving tour on a 4.9-mile one-way loop road takes visitors to these and six other battle sites. For information phone 417-732-2662.

Walnut Street Inn

Springfield, Missouri

Its location at the entrance to the Ozarks made Springfield a military objective in the war. Confederates took it over in the Battle of Wilson's Creek, but Union forces recaptured it the next year and kept it, turning back numerous Confederate attacks.

Wild Bill Hickok was a scout and spy for Union forces headquartered here. The **Springfield National Cemetery,** on Seminole St., has the graves of 1,514 Union soldiers, some seven hundred of them unknown, lost at Wilson's Creek and other battles in the area. The **Confederate Cemetery,** established in 1870, has 463 gravesites, some of which hold unknown soldiers.

The Walnut Street Inn, once known as the McCann-Jewell house, is one of the few remaining Victorian Gothic houses in Springfield. Charles McCann, who built the house for his young bride, went on to become one of the four largest wagon makers in the country. Harry S. Jewell, a later owner, was a prominent newspaper publisher.

Turn-of-the-century elegance and hospitality explain why *Country Inns* magazine chose it as one of the top twelve inns in the country. All of the guest rooms are furnished with antiques, and some feature a whirlpool bath and stocked bar, and all have cable TV. Two doors away is the satellite Cottage Inn with three additional suites. Breakfast is a delight, with Ozark treats like piping hot persimmon muffins, warm walnut bread, and freshly squeezed orange juice chilled to perfection.

Address: 900 E. Walnut St., Springfield, MO 65806;
  tel: 417-864-6346 or 800-593-6346; fax: 417-864-6184;
  E-mail: walnutstinnepcis.net.
Accommodations: Six guest rooms in the main house, four in the carriage house, and two suites in the Cottage Inn, all with private baths.
Amenities: Air-conditioning, off-street parking, bathrobes, phones and cable TV in rooms.
Rates: $$–$$$. Major credit cards and personal checks.
Restrictions: No pets, no smoking.

Garth Woodside Mansion

Hannibal, Missouri

There's a fort just outside of town where Union troops guarded the railroad, but most people don't come to Hannibal to see that. They come to see the boyhood home of a young man who after three weeks as a recruit in the Confederate army deserted and went West.

That boy, Samuel Clemens, found fame as Mark Twain, and made Hannibal famous with two books, *The Adventures of Tom Sawyer* and *The Adventures of Huckleberry Finn.*

Many years later Twain's company published the memoirs of Ulysses S. Grant, who was nearly broke and dying of throat cancer, and earned over $450,000 in royalties for Mrs. Grant.

This inn is the Second Empire mansion where in 1882 Twain stayed with his boyhood friend John Garth when he returned to Hannibal. Some say Garth was one of the models for Tom Sawyer. In 1988, when Irv and Diane Feinberg made the house an inn, they retained many of its original furnishings.

The inn has a flying staircase that vaults three stories without visible means of support, an impressive library, and the room where Mark Twain slept. The inn provides guests with nineteenth-century nightshirts, which may be worn not only for sleeping but also at breakfast.

Address: RR 3, Box 578, Hannibal, MO 63401;
tel: 573-221-2789; E-mail: garthenemonet.com.
Accommodations: Eight double rooms, all with private baths.
Amenities: Air-conditioning, off-street parking, afternoon refreshments, fishing on the property.
Rates: $$. Visa, MasterCard, and personal checks.
Restrictions: No children under twelve, no pets, restricted smoking.

Index

About the Author

CHUCK LAWLISS grew up in Vermont listening to his relatives swap Civil War stories. Three of his great-great grandfathers fought in the war, including one who was a prisoner for eighteen months at Andersonville, the notorious Confederate prison camp.

He is the author of the bestselling *Civil War Sourcebook and Travel Guide* (Harmony Books) and has written many magazine and newspaper articles on various aspects of the war. He is currently researching historic inns and sites of the Revolutionary War for a book to be called *George Washington Slept Here*.

Mr. Lawliss was a newspaper and magazine journalist for many years, writing for the Associated Press, *New York Herald Tribune*, *Holiday Magazine*, and *Art In America*. He lives in Philadelphia.

Don't miss Jeff Shaara's
NEW YORK TIMES bestselling saga
of the Civil War . . .
Gods and Generals

"Brilliant does not even begin to describe the Shaara gift.

Thank *Gods and Generals* that it was passed
from father to son."
—*Atlanta Journal-Constitution*

. . . Or the stunning sequel to
the Pulitzer Prize–winning classic
The Killer Angels
The Last Full Measure

Coming to bookstores in June 1998!
Published by the Ballantine Publishing Group